The Chelson is awarded to state competition winners who's works stand out nationally as exceptional publications based on content, originality and writing professionalism.

The Chelson is awarded annually to the six most distinguished literary talents of the year in the fields of Fiction, Poetry, Inspiration and Technology by the Association for Literary Arts, a division of 1st World Library - Literary Society.

Miracles cease to be called miracles when they occur with regularity. Here's what some have said about the author and "How to: Have a Nice Day." We hope you'll send us your story too!

After 17 years of emergency rooms, doctors, psychiatrists, pain, depression and many, many medications I have finally found relief. I am Having a Nice Day, everyday. Thank you, Gary.

Jason Gay, Irrigation Engineer; Tarpon Springs, Fl.

I earn over $1 million dollars per year and Gary has been one of my teachers. I am Having a Nice Day, everyday. Thank you, Gary

Shawn Casey, author, www.ShawnCasey.com; Duluth, Ga.

A buldging disc has aggravated me for many years and I was told surgery was the only answer. My world has opened in so many ways since reading Gary's book. Now, I am pain free and Having a very Nice Day. Thank you, Gary.

Phyllis Cole, Mgr. Insurance Industry; Tarpon Springs, Fl.

After 27 years of Multiple Sclerosis the symptoms are miraculously regressing and I am finally Having a Nice Day. Chapter 5 has changed my life. Thank you, Gary

Sandra Kischuk, www.LivingBeyondLimits.com and former IBM Project Mgr.; Tampa. Fl.

I've purchased four copies of Gary's book. Why? Because the greatest gift I can give is health, happiness, and peace. Thank you, Gary

Susan Sexauer, Animal Behavioral Specialist, Tampa, Fl.

I had experienced debilitating migraine headaches without any relief or hope in sight. Once again I am enjoying a pain free productive life and I am Having a Nice Day, everyday. Thank you, Gary

Hank Seitz, CEO www.epicsuccess.com; Tampa, Fl.

Whether you're just coming to matters of the spirit or are a seasoned "seeker" this book will delight you. Gary reminds us of many significant universal truths and adds some of his own, the result of which promotes both inner and world peace and harmony.

Dr. Terra Pressler, Author, Professor; Santa Fe, New Mexico.

What Dr. Norman Vincent Peale's "Power of Positive Thinking" was to our past, Gary's "How to: Have a Nice Day" is to our future. It has changed my life and I am confident will change the world. I am happy. Thank you, Gary.

Vilma Riesgo, Retired, Former Dean of Students; Tampa, Fl.

I had no idea the power I was wasting. This book will be valuable to women and men everywhere. Life is good. I am happy. Thank you, Gary.

Linda Burhans, Founder www.ProfessionalWomen-Empower.org; St. Petersburg, Fl.

Several conditions were interfering with my living a happy life. After working with Gary's techniques they are now much improved and I am back to Having a Nice Day, every day. Thank you, Gary

Mary Barbara, Founder St. Petersburg Course in Miracles Center; St. Petersburg, Fl.

Please know that I am not easy to please with books. This is a GOOD one. I loved it. I don't know another self-help book like this one. I've been around a long time, and I've read a lot of books. Since I minored in psychology, quite naturally, I thought I knew it all. "How to: Have a Nice Day" was more than a delightful surprise. There was a surprise on every page. A new angle, something revealed in a new light, things I never knew before, never thought of before, and I needed them all. I've never seen the likes of this book. It's easy to read, FUN, profound and bold. Not a quick-fix, but my day did get better. There are two exercises in this book that blew me away. Don't miss them. This is a healing book. It healed my heart. Reading this book is being in the company of the wise. I give this book 5 Stars.

Gloria Wendroff, author of Love Letters From God, www.heavenletters.org; Fairfield, Iowa

For many years I experienced depression, fear, anxiety, an inability to sleep, and resultantly alcoholism. I had even been confined as a danger to myself. Naturally, I had "tried" many conventional methods and medications, obviously without success. Now, the constant fear is gone; the depression has lifted; and I have not had any re-occurrence for nearly two years. Yes, I am Having a very Nice Day. Thank you, Gary.

Scott P. Casey, Internet Marketing Consultant; Knoxville, Tenn.

A love issue from my childhood was repeatedly impacting my relationships. Ultimately, I experienced diverticulosis. It is gone. I am medication free and Having a very Nice Day. Thank you, Gary

Carol Mitchell, Singer/Songwriter; St. Petersburg, Fl.

How to :
Have a Nice Day

Gary Schineller

Creator of "Hello, From My Heart" Day
Proven to be: A day that changed the World.

1st WORLD
PUBLISHING

How to Have a Nice Day

Gary Schineller

© Gary Schineller 2004

Published by 1stWorld Publishing
1100 North 4th St. Suite 131, Fairfield, Iowa 52556
TEL: 641-209-5000 • FAX: 641-209-3001
•WEB: www.1stworldpublishing.com

First Edition

LCCN: 2004099576
SoftCover ISBN: 1-59540-910-6
HardCover ISBN: 1-59540-914-9
eBook ISBN: 1-59540-913-0

Cover Design - Sharon Bond,
Zebra Graphics (941) 708-2970

To live
is
to love

How to Have a Nice Day has been lovingly edited
by Dr Terra Pressler
I am eternally grateful

Table of Contents

Power Quiz

— • • —

The following is your Personal Power Quiz. I invite you to record your answers. There's another copy of this quiz after the last chapter. You'll want to record your answers then also and compare them to those you record now. The changes you notice will serve as your reminder of "How to: Have a Nice Day."

Mark the answer that most clearly represents your belief. **Please remember there are no wrong answers.**

1. (a) I always have a good day.
   (b) I always try to make it a good day.
   (c) I have no control over whether or not I have a good day.

2. (a) I hate one person.
   (b) I hate a few people.
   (c) I don't hate anyone.

3   (a) I am a happy person.

     (b) I try to be a happy person.

     (c) I get mad once in a while.

4   (a) I feel worried about the future.

     (b) I live in the moment and am grateful.

     (c) I wish I could turn back the clock.

5   (a) I have the courage to fight for my convictions.

     (b) I like to remain neutral.

     (c) I believe in equality.

6   (a) I get sick once in a while.

     (b) I am always perfect.

     (c) I have a recurring condition.

7   (a) I am always on time.

     (b) I am sorry when I arrive late.

     (c) I don't care if I am late.

8   (a) I sometimes worry about money

     (b) I always have enough money.

     (c) I don't care about money.

9   (a) My life can sometimes be described as " Why does this keep happening to me?"

     (b) I look at all events as happening for me versus to me.

     (c) I desire a healthy relationship.

Gary Schineller

10 (a) What others think of me has nothing to do with what I think of myself.

(b) I am willing to look at things from other's point of view.

(c) I feel guilty or ashamed once in a while

About the Author

— —

*G*ary Schineller has proven a way to create a happier, healthier, and more peaceful community. What he has proven for society can and does work for each and every one of us. Individual benefits will result in happier, more successful relationships both personally and in business.

Many of us can recall people and relationships which were significant in our development. Gary recalls his Uncle Andre. He was not related, but one of his dad's closest friends. He was also one of the brightest individuals Gary ever had the pleasure of knowing.

Andre had been born to the Russian Aristocracy, but courtesy of the Bolshevik revolution, became a refugee and traveled the world. Only, everywhere Andre went he learned the language. Gary recalls his Uncle Andre spoke and wrote over thirteen languages fluently. They included two dialects of Chinese, Japanese, all the romance languages, German, Polish, Greek, even Swahili, and of course Russian and English.

Gary was greatly impressed by what he found to be the simple loving wisdom of Andre. He looked forward to every time they got together. He knew Andre would challenge him intellectually and he wanted to show he was up to the task. Part of the way Gary would do this was to learn the longest "fifty-cent" words he could master. Then he would try to use them in a sentence with Uncle Andre.

That is, until one day. This was one of those days where he had maybe a "seventy-five" cent word. Gary was about age nine at the time.

Well, he found a way to work this word into conversation. It doesn't matter what the word was. Because, right after this triumphant moment, Andre placed his hand on Gary's shoulder. He lovingly looked into his eyes and softly said, "When you really know what you are talking about, the words will be this big!" As Andre said this he held his

Gary Schineller

thumb and fore-finger very, very close!

Gary never forgot that. He will forever be grateful for all of his father's close friends, especially Uncle Andre. That lesson, taught so many years ago, is evident in "How To: Have A Nice Day."

Gary has spent most of his award winning career in broadcast television in Buffalo, Chicago, Detroit and New York City. During this time he was named New York State Volunteer of the Year for his work with the American Heart Association.

He became ordained by the Universal Brotherhood Movement in 1999, has taught many self-realization classes, and has been a guest pastor at many churches. He has also participated in many miracles of healing. While every individual miracle is significant, the most grand was his 2002 creation of "Hello, From My Heart" Day in Tampa Bay, Florida. Through the simple exchange of that greeting by an estimated 750,000 people, crime was dramatically lowered by 22% throughout the eight counties of Tampa Bay on August 1, 2002.

The reader might also be interested in knowing that August 1st was Gary's father's birthday. Since he does not believe in coincidences, this is quite fitting.

He has also founded an organization known as COMMA. This is a non-denominational association of individuals committed to creating a happier, healthier, more peaceful community. It is his philosophy that all of us are ministers. Only some of us have chosen to be ordained. This represents the membership of COMMA.

Given Gary's patriotic nature his dream will sound familiar: *e pluribus unum*. Out of many, one!

Dedications

—◆—

Marissa and Amelia Schineller, my daughters. Before they were born I thought I knew about love. At their birth I realized I had just scratched the surface. They have taught me more than they will ever know.

William J. Schineller, my dad. He taught me to follow my heart.

Linda Lou Rodgers, my friend. Her unconditional love made this book possible.

Introduction

—◦—

$\mathcal{F}$irst, there are no secrets. What you are now reading will often feel like you already know it. It's true, you do! This book simply brings it to consciousness. As students of the philosophy of mind we call that "raising your vibration." Have you ever felt a wave of tingling or goose-bumps come over your body? We know these to be CB's or confirmation bumps. They are a signal of truth.

Who will benefit from this work? The world. Yes, I'll explain. The information herein contained will benefit our society, our global civilization, every teacher, preacher and person. Certain elements are brand new. If written elsewhere, I have not been exposed to their concepts. In all the books I have read, and lectures and services I have attended, I have never seen all of these practices in action. Yet, I have met no one who does not agree with their validity.

One element is certain, you will be forever changed. It is reported that by the time you finish this work you will be happier, healthier, and more at peace. You will also have a new-found power and strength. And every day that you practice for one month, two months, etc., your strength and connection to the universe will be that much more advanced. The physical reality of more abundant health and happiness will be the manifestation of your new strength.

Let us begin.

I tried very hard not to write this book. That's right, I tried not to write this book. Many of you who are reading this will know instantly what I mean. It seems the laws of physics, the laws of nature do operate on many planes. We've all heard that for every action there is an equal and opposite reaction. Most of us, however, did not expect this to apply to our individual evolution.

I don't know why. We just didn't expect it.

Well, I'm here to testify. The higher you raise your vibration, the more forces will present themselves to perform "an equal and opposite reaction."

A lot of you are aware of this and continue to successfully battle these forces. Many more of us, however, are not aware of these forces which result in lives which resemble the pattern of a sine wave; i.e. filled with ups and downs. These ups and downs represent tests. Have you ever heard someone say, "Why does this keep happening to me?" Of course you have. At times you may have said this yourself. Congratulations, you have just taken the first step in raising your vibration! You are aware, or as some say you are waking up. This awareness is like a test. You will be given the same test over and over until you pass. That's why we say events do not happen to us, they happen for us. Then, when that same occurrence transpires, it will no longer be a test. You will have graduated… from that challenge.

If we respond to the same challenge or test in the same way, relax; we are bound to receive what might be called a make-up exam. This will be discussed in greater and more specific detail in Chapter Nine.

What are some of the common ways to lower your

vibration! How about booze, drugs, television, tobacco? Most of you will agree with the chemical/dulling reaction that booze, drugs and tobacco cause on the brain. We all know they can even kill us. (Now, that's a real termination of our vibration.) But, television as well as any addictive occupation which results in passivity will by its very nature depress this vibration. Key to this is two words: addiction and passivity. Most things in moderation are fine.

Passivity when dealing with hatred, guilt, shame, greed, fear and anger will also lower our vibration. We've all experienced one or all of these. While at the moment of expression we might feel powerful, it is a false power. These emotions or attitudes actually lower our power, and decrease our joy. As we learn to be intentional with our behavior, our joy will rise to previously unfound levels. In this process we also gain many new friends.

The title of this work was given to me approximately six years ago. What do I mean by that? Have you ever been complimented on your creativity? Of course you have. Where do you think your creativity comes from? I think it's a gift which comes from God or Spirit. Did I write this book six years ago? Of course not. Four years ago a young woman came to me after having been diagnosed terminal

Gary Schineller

with HIV. I am also a practicing Reiki Master. Reiki is a discipline of healing which is spiritually based and energy-driven. It is also now practiced in most major hospitals. Three weeks after we began working together she decided to stop taking all medication. Three months later her doctors were unable to find the virus in her blood. Her treatment consisted of Reiki, Contemplative Intention and a uniquely applied study of the I AM. She now had the tools to release the virus and lead a happy life on a daily basis. The I AM will be described in Chapter One.

By the way, I have long since stopped believing my own press releases. This was not "me" providing the healing. I was merely the vehicle. My message concerning this gift was to share it. To write a book. Did I write this book then? Nope! Four months later I felt called upon to teach a class on this subject and did so for eight months at the Harmony Church in Tampa, Fl. All who attended remarked how these teachings changed their lives with greater peace, happiness, and health. Did I write this book then?

Not yet!

My contract with a television network was not renewed by the new president of the company. This gave me more time to write this book. Did I? Not yet; but I'm now nine months from today. Friends at a cable channel called and asked if I would create and host a one hour special on healing. I did. That was two months ago.

So you see, I had many reminders, many sources of encouragement, many blessings, and many tests. Clearly, none of them were coincidences! I then wrote for six months and stopped. I didn't know the reason then, but I do now! I needed to create a day that would change the World. And that day was August 1st 2002, the first "Hello, From My Heart" Day.

This is one of my favorite jokes. I think you'll find it appropriate. I think you'll also appreciate its humor in your life. "Do you know how to make God laugh?" The answer is: "Tell him your plans!" Like I said, I tried very hard not to write this book. I hope you like it.

Gary Schineller

Preface

＊—＊

*T*he *Desiderata* was discovered in the 1600's in the Abby of Old St. Paul's Church in Baltimore, Md., USA. No one knows who actually wrote it. However, I find there is not a life question that is not answered within it.

Personally, I wonder who is smiling right now because they remember seeing and reading it in someone's home or office. You see, I am a sort of Johnny Appleseed of the *Desiderata* and have for many years distributed it to homes and offices across America. For those in crisis, I recommend reading it daily.

It is my belief that we are all ministers. Some of us have chosen to be ordained. However, each and every one of us has helped or counseled another to help them gain peace and happiness.

I present it to you now so that you might have it whenever you feel a need. Its contents, especially when read out loud, will assist you to work through any challenge.

Desiderata

Go placidly amid the noise and the haste, and remember what peace there may be in silence. As far as possible, without surrender, be on good terms with all persons. Speak your truth quietly and clearly; and listen to others, even to the dull and ignorant; they too have their story. Avoid loud and aggressive persons; they are vexations to the spirit. If you compare yourself to others, you may become vain or bitter, for always there will be greater and lesser persons than yourself. Enjoy your achievements as well as your plans. Keep interested in your own career, however humble; it is a real possession in the changing fortunes of time. Exercise caution in your business affairs, for the world is full of trickery. But let this not blind you to what virtue there is; many persons strive for high ideals, and everywhere life is full of heroism. Be yourself. Especially do not feign affection. Neither be

Gary Schineller

cynical about love; for in the face of all aridity and disen-
chantment it is perennial as the grass. Take kindly the
counsel of years, gracefully surrendering the things of
youth. Nurture strength of spirit to shield you in sudden
misfortune. But do not distress yourself with dark imaginings. Many fears are born of fatigue and loneliness.
Beyond a wholesome discipline, be gentle with yourself.
You are a child of the universe no less than the trees and
the stars; you have a right to be here. And whether or
not it is clear to you, no doubt the universe is unfolding
as it should. Therefore be at peace with God, whatever
you conceive Him to be. And whatever your labours and
aspirations, in the noisy confusion of life, keep peace in
your soul. With all its sham, drudgery and broken
dreams, it is still a
Beautiful world.
Be cheerful.
Strive to be happy.

1.

I AM

—•—

I am. How many times would you say you have said these two seemingly little words in your lifetime; how many times today? Think about it? While you're considering your answer here's an appropriate healing story.

Since moving to Florida, its only natural that friends from the Northland visit, especially in the winter. Most don't realize that Florida experiences winter also. There are a seemingly unpredictable number of days when the temperature reaches a high in the 60's and drops down to the 30's at night. This naturally affects the water temperature. On one of those days, I met my friends on a beach in St. Petersburg. April was experiencing severe problems with one knee. It was swollen to three times its size and she had been told it would require surgery. First, we meditated and two answers were given. One was for her to consider what new steps she was not taking in her life. This, by the way, is often the case when there is an injury or condition afflicting one's leg or foot. It's usually a signal that we may be stuck in a rut. By continuing to do things the way we always have, we will get the same results. If this rings true with you, you probably already know the next step. Let this be your invitation to take it. The other message I received for April was to perform Reiki and go in the water. I performed Reiki and we walked to the water's edge.

Now, in some ways this lady might be characterized as a "pretty-sissy." We all know people like that. It's not judgement, just description. I genuinely love April. Well, the water temperature was 53 degrees Fahrenheit. You can easily predict her answer: "I am not going in there!" We looked into each other's eyes as we repeated several times together: "I AM warm." Thirty minutes later we got out of the water. We had walked, waist high for thirty minutes. I even swam awhile. When we emerged her knee was almost normal in size!

Now, back to my question. What's your answer? How many times a day do you say I am trying; I am sorry; I am sick; I am mad, sad, or angry or any of the other colorful words we have available. Would you change your answer now? Probably. Will you now reflect on how powerful you can be when you say "I am _____." Experiment for a moment. Think about how you want to feel. Perhaps you might say: "I am happy". Repeat it out loud several times and say it from your heart. It works, doesn't it?

Now, I'll tell you why. There are actually two disciplines that support this reality. They are spirituality and physics. They can work separately or together. We can choose one or both.

First, let's explore spirituality. In the second book of Moses when asked His name God replied: "I AM, That I Am." And we learned in Genesis that we are created in God's image. Hence, we recognize the God presence within all of us. Therefore, when we are saying I AM, we are technically saying God is. It doesn't get more powerful than that. A word of caution: lest you take the name of

God in vain you are encouraged to think about how you now complete your God is _____, or I am _____ sentences. But, more on that later.

If you subscribe to this discipline, consider the following:

I AM trying	God is trying
I AM afraid	God is afraid
I AM sick	God is sick
I AM worried	God is worried
I AM angry	God is angry
I AM mad	God is mad
I AM ashamed	God is ashamed
I AM sorry	God is sorry

Is God any of these things?

I'll ask again. Would you take the name of God in vain? I am sure you would not, not knowingly. Remember, we are very powerful, and gaining more power every day. When we pay attention to this discipline, we are happier, healthier, and more joyous.

Gary Schineller

By the way, do you know the definition of an atheist? He is someone without invisible means of support! I have proven the power of the I AM. Medical Science has also proven the power of prayer. Hundreds of studies support this. Many have been published and appear in the May 2001 issue of Readers Digest. They also report that individuals who attend some form of religious service more than once a week live an average of seven years longer than those who do not.

At an early age I was taught that we can enjoy the experience of being at a religious service whenever and wherever we are. Being intentional and disciplined with our thoughts and words is one way of achieving this benefit.

In Physics we deal with patterns. Patterns are predictably repeatable. That's why Physics is a science. Our thoughts create energy patterns. The application of them is called manifestation. The trained mind can manifest very easily. Most of us, however, send enumerable mixed messages. That's what we are going to focus on in this work. We are all very powerful. We always have been. We may have been even more powerful in our youth. Our minds were perhaps more clear. We shall regain that and more.

Here's a short story about the power of thought. I'm one of those 60's generation types who put himself through college. Yes, I was a hippie. Naturally, funds were scarce. And the desire to party was, shall I say normal. I also had an average-plus talent for pool. Therefore, I would find myself with my buddies visiting various neighborhood taverns. Most pubs in Buffalo, N.Y. had pool tables. Buffalo also boasted a statistic I've never confirmed, but seems plausible enough: there are more bars per capita in that city than any other in the country. In my mind then, this was perfect. Back to the pool game. Usually, we would play for beers, sometimes a small wager. Keep in mind that my talent was okay, not great, and my pockets were certainly not deep. Well, I found that if my opponent, who perhaps might be an excellent player, was bearing down on even the simplest shot to win the game, I could concentrate and send energy to the back of his brain. That energy or thought was that he would miss the shot. Depending on the hour of the evening, or how many games I had already won, my opponent almost always missed.

Here's something I've found more and more people experiencing. Have you ever answered the telephone and

Gary Schineller

known who was calling before they said hello? Do you think this is a coincidence? I don't.

When I am asked to speak to a congregation or other group, I enjoy this demonstration. I call it "The Eyes of Love." First, I divide the group in half. The left side of the room gets the hard job. They have to look at me! The right side gets to close their eyes. Next, I instruct those on the left side to each turn and face someone on the right. Hopefully, they each pick different people. Now, I ask them to concentrate on sending love to the person they are looking at. After several moments I instruct the right side, with their eyes still closed, to turn their heads until they feel they are face to face with eyes of love. Having done that everyone opens their eyes. I then ask for a show of hands to measure their success. The smallest percentage was 80%. Many groups score 100%.

So you see, whether we are spiritual or not, we have a gift. Using it wisely for the Greatest Good is how we shall proceed.

2.

In the Beginning........
the Source of Our Power

---

*S*ome might wonder why is this Chapter Two. After all, the beginning is the beginning, isn't it? Well, not really. Most of us grew up with a blind understanding that the creation consisted of the heavens, the earth, light, water, and Adam and Eve. Obviously, Adam was created in God's image and Eve was that whole rib thing.

Actually, Adam and Eve don't appear on the scene until Chapter Two of Genesis. In this Chapter, after the seventh day, God formed man from the dust and breathed life into his nostrils and then he became a living thing.

So, what about Chapter One and why am I suddenly dwelling on all this Biblical stuff? After all, this book is called "How to: Have a Nice Day." It's because we need a common understanding of our power. How else can we respect it? How else can we use it? And most important, what do we do with it when we've got it? Most of us really, I mean really, don't know what makes us happy. With a common understanding, a sense of Oneness will develop within you, wherein all things are possible.

It's important for me to digress for a moment longer at this point. To me faith is personal. Mine is very strong. Our purpose here is not to sell you my faith or anyone elses. Our purpose is for each and every one of you to genuinely and gloriously have a really nice day.

Now, back to Genesis, Chapter One. Here it is written, "Let Us make man in Our image, according to Our likeness...So God created man in His own image, male and female He created them." Since form was only introduced in Chapter Two, we may conclude that initially we were created as energy which is also the image of God. Ah

Gary Schineller

hah (Dear reader, this might be one of those times you are feeling a sense of tingling emerging through all or part of your body.).

There is only one other passage, also from Genesis, which I find key to our mutual understanding. It is one that I pondered for over twenty years! Since I feel that a lot of the Bible is allegory, I knew there had to be a deeper meaning than the surface interpretation of the Tower of Babel. For those that don't recall, as children many of us were taught that this story was an explanation for the many languages on the planet.

I asked many what they thought this passage might really be about. Now, don't get me wrong. This was not the type of burning question that consumes your every waking thought. Rather, this was a question which periodically and perpetually would return to my consciousness. No one had an answer for me. Then one morning while jogging around the N.Y.C. harbor in what is called the Bay Ridge section of Brooklyn, an answer came. It seems especially appropriate that this particular morning it was very, very foggy. Visibility was maybe twenty-five feet. Emerging from the fog, I began to see glimpses of a huge column, like stone. As I marveled, almost in awe, at what at the time seemed like a vision, I felt an awakening. Some of you, I know, can relate to this. It's like having a memory that analytically you have no business knowing. Some call it Déjà Vu. Here's how it unfolded. God created these marvelous machines we call our bodies. All of science marvels at the amazing intricacy of our bodies and how perfectly they work.

However, science also agrees that we only use about 10% of our brains. Do you think we were created that way? I don't!

The message given to me while running in the fog was that we used to have full use of our brains. With that we didn't need spoken language. We had the ability to communicate telepathically. We also had full knowledge of all our past lives, and profound abilities of manifestation. That's why man at that time lived for hundreds of years. Yet, we abused these gifts by attempting to construct the Tower of Babel wherein we would "make a name for ourselves" in heaven. Our gifts were taken away. I have presented this information to a number of Biblical scholars who unanimously concur with the plausibility of this explanation.

Gary Schineller

At this time you might like to consider the great Pyramids. No one yet understands how they could have been constructed. Do you suppose the Egyptians had a greater use of their complete brains?

The good news is what's happening now. You are reading this book.

Chances are you have or will read others also aimed at raising your consciousness. Time magazine has reported in recent years that nearly three fourths of us believe in angels and an astounding two thirds of us say some form of grace before a meal. Look at television. Today, there are programs like "Touched by an Angel," "Mysterious Ways," "Unsolved Mysteries," "It's a Miracle," "Oprah," and many more. Hollywood insiders have told me the current buzzword for new projects is "Spiritual Action Adventures." The momentum is building. Our thirst for answers is growing and the entertainment industry, naturally, seeks to satisfy it.

Where will this lead? In the 60's we talked about getting back to the Garden. We are on our way!

There is one more bit of information that bears illumination regarding The Tower of Babel. I described the Déjà

Vu like experience while running in the fog. Remember that huge stone column which appeared to rise up through the fog? This was the trigger for my revelation. We all experience triggers. However, we do not always let the message come through. Often we approach these experiences with our left brain, our analytical side. The alternative is to allow yourself to employ the right side of your brain, your intuitive or feeling side. This is particularly easy for women to develop, and more difficult for men.

I remember my early classes in beginning meditation. The women were seeing colors, seeing angels and getting messages. It seemed the more I, and the rest of the men "tried," the more unsuccessful we were. It's okay. It's normal. We men have been raised to be more analytical and less trusting of our feelings. However, in recent years due, I think, to the collective consciousness being raised, through increased meditating, and more people seeking and finding their spiritual answers all peoples, men included, are opening up quickly. It's not unusual for a man to achieve color and other visualization in his first meditation. That's right, what took me years to achieve is now commonly achieved in a first experience.

There is a well known research story which confirms

Gary Schineller

the power of collective consciousness. It's called the 100th Monkey.

100th MONKEY

The Japanese monkey, Macaca fuscata, has been observed in the wild for a period of over thirty years.

In 1952, on the island of Koshima, scientists were providing monkeys with sweet potatoes dropped in the sand. The monkeys liked the taste of the raw sweet potatoes, but they found the dirt unpleasant.

An eighteen-month-old female named Imo found she could solve the problem by washing the potatoes in a nearby stream. She taught this trick to her mother. Her playmates also learned this new way and they taught their mothers, too.

This cultural innovation was gradually picked up by various monkeys before the eyes of the scientists. Between 1952 and 1958 all the young monkeys learned to wash the sandy sweet potatoes to make them more palatable.

Only the adults who imitated their children learned this social improvement. Other adults kept eating the dirty sweet potatoes. Then something startling took place. In the autumn of 1958, a certain number of Koshima monkeys were washing sweet potatoes--the exact number is not known.

Let us suppose that when the sun rose one morning there were ninety-nine monkeys on Koshima Island who had learned to wash their sweet potatoes. Let's further suppose that later that morning the hundredth monkey learned to wash potatoes.

THEN IT HAPPENED!

By that evening almost everyone in the tribe was washing sweet potatoes before eating them. The added energy of this hundredth monkey somehow created an ideological breakthrough. But notice: the most surprising thing observed by these scientists was that the habit of washing sweet potatoes then spontaneously jumped over the sea ---

Colonies of monkeys on other islands and the mainland troop of monkeys at Takasakiyama began washing their sweet potatoes. Thus, when a certain critical number achieves an awareness, this new awareness may be communicated from mind to mind.

Although the exact number may vary, the Hundredth Monkey Phenomenon means that when only a limited number of people know of a new way, it may remain the consciousness property of these people. But there is a

Gary Schineller

point at which if only one more person tunes in to a new awareness, a field is strengthened so that this awareness reaches almost everyone!

The experiments of Dr. J. B. Rhine at Duke University repeatedly demonstrated that individuals can communicate private information to each other even though located in different places. We now know that the strength of this extrasensory communication can be amplified to a powerfully effective level when the consciousness of the "hundredth person" is added. You may be the "Hundredth Person".....

If you've ever wanted to participate in saving the planet, you are. That's right, you already are. Think about it. If you "have a nice day" and someone else does and someone else and so on, what will happen? We have proved this in Tampa, Florida with "Hello, From My Heart" Day (More on that later) It's fun, isn't it?

Lots of us like to chart our progress. In addition to your meditative experiences, here's a way. On the back outside cover you'll find a chart. Now, locate a timepiece with a sweep second hand. Wait for it to reach the zero point. When it does, begin reading the chart aloud. However, instead of saying the word, say the color. For example the first word says YELLOW, but it is in green. Therefore, you will say green, and so on. Remember to time yourself. Now, see your results on the next page.

(TO SEE THIS CHART IN COLOR PLEASE TURN TO THE BACK COVER)

Look at the chart and say the <u>COLOR</u> not the word

YELLOW BLUE ORANGE
BLACK RED GREEN
PURPLE YELLOW RED
ORANGE GREEN BLACK
BLUE RED PURPLE
GREEN BLUE ORANGE

Left – Right Conflict
Your right brain tries to say the color but your left brain insists on reading the word.

How long did it take you?

Gary Schineller

The following is a chart of students with their average score:

Telepath	:05 - :10
Psychic	:10 - :15
Gifted	:15 - :20
Open	:20 - :25
Opening	:25 - :30
Pathfinder	:30+

As you do the work in this book, as you have more and more nice days, retake this test and chart your progress.

3.

Spiritual Attachments

—◆ ◆—

Spiritual Attachments are a fact of life. They always have been. Those of us living in urban areas are at the greatest risk. Here's what I am talking about. When someone dies a violent or confused death, e.g., from murder, accident, alcohol, drugs, etc., their spirit is often confused. It naturally seeks the light, just like a moth to a flame, but in its dazed state it may confuse one of our lights with Divine Light. Yes, each of us possess a Divine Light. It is also measurable.

All of us have a light. You've perhaps heard of your

aura. Well, that's your light. Those of you who are gifted can see it without aid. Otherwise, you can seek out a shop or store which is equipped with an Auraphotography or Kirilian Photography machine. All of us can also, measure the strength of our energy with a pendulum. This will be explained in detail later.

One of the more famous examples of Spiritual Attachment concerns a perfectly normal young man in his early twenties. He was leading a normal, productive, happy life. One morning as he stepped out of his front door, a car driving down the road in front of his house struck a tree and the driver was killed instantly. Inside of thirty days our perfectly normal young man became an alcoholic. He lost his job and his girlfriend. It seems the driver was an alcoholic. Once this connection was established, our young man was cleared of the attachment and he resumed his happy life.

Sometimes spirits hang around for other reasons. Here's another example. I was involved in the clearing of a very troubled young woman in her late thirties. She came to a Church class I was teaching and looked extremely haggard. Her face was drawn. Her eyes revealed a fear and frustration which had become her daily life. She described

Gary Schineller

being unable to have a normal relationship. She described feeling as though her body was being violated. Her days and nights were consumed with these violations. She had been experiencing this for years. She had been to many doctors and psychiatrists and was coming to us as a last resort. She didn't know if she could take it any more and she was desperate. Healing, I thought would be easy. We would first smudge her. That's where you move the smoke of sage around the entire body. You start under the soles of the feet and work your way around the entire body, arms, legs and head. The cleansing power of sage has been used since ancient times. It is still used in many conventional or traditional churches today, although many appear to have forgotten why. After we cleansed her with sage, we performed Reiki, blessed the spirit, and released it to the light. Then we prayed to fill the void, now created, with love. The transformation on her face was remarkable. Everyone marveled. She felt relief and peace for the first time in years. We, naturally, felt a great satisfaction.

I eagerly looked forward to seeing her at next week's class. When she entered, she was a wreck again! Oh, boy, this was not what I expected. A brief interview provided an answer. After last weeks class she had felt better than she had in years. It lasted until she went to bed. That was it! Her home was inhabited, and they had not been invited. Simple, I thought: smudge the home. This is done by taking a smoking smudge pot of sage completely around the ceiling perimeter of every room and around every window and every doorway. First we cleared her in class again and meditated as before. My little army then proceeded to her home. The smudging was done. She had a wonderful night's rest. Another week went by as I awaited her entrance to class.

You guessed it. Once again she entered a total wreck. All the haggardness of her appearance had returned. It's rare, but I felt indignant. So I asked two questions: what she did for a living and for how long had she experienced these violations? She answered: "I own an estate jewelry shop I've been suffering for nearly eleven years!" I replied: "Let me guess how long you've owned this business....11 years?" She looked at me with an incredulous, open-mouth stare as she wondered out loud: "How did you know?" We repeated all the steps of the past two weeks and instructed her to smudge her shop and all the pieces within it. Also, she was to smudge any new purchases for her shop before she brought them inside. She has been fine ever since. Yes,

Gary Schineller

confused spirits can linger for many reasons. In this case some of the estate jewelry was the conduit for her attachment.

All of my guided meditations, healing groups, and healing sessions begin the same way. Everyone is smudged. I encourage you to do the same. After this I also suggest that you say a prayer. In this prayer, which needs to be of your own design, it is important to ask for angelic help to guide you in performing work that is for the Greatest Good. If you are a beginner at this, you may want to enlist the aid of an experienced practitioner. If you call for the Archangels, they will come. I promise.

Many who are on a spiritual path will call this work exorcism. For all intents and purposes it is the same. The Catholic Church has responded to this growing societal need with heretofore unprecedented action. They now employ twenty full-time exorcists nationwide. Several years ago they employed one for the entire United States. Most are in urban areas.

Recently, I was asked to work with a young man of 33 who suffered from depression. He had been hospitalized many times and seen many doctors. Apparently, the depression was triggered by very intense chest pains. The pains were so intense they resembled those of a heart attack. Incredibly, he had been enduring these since the age of sixteen. Every drug possible had been prescribed, all without any effect except temporary relief. Needless to say, his quality of life was not what you would call happy! I began to explore what took place in his life at the time when the pains first started. Low and behold in our second session I learned that he, one of his brothers, and a teacher had experimented with the occult and a Ouija Board when he was sixteen. That was the answer. After only three Spiritual Counseling sessions, and smudging his home, seventeen years of pain and suffering have finally stopped.

Let this be a warning to any who wish to play with the occult, Ouija boards, and the like. If you notice someone who suddenly displays basic personality changes. This may be a sign of an attachment. You may wish to consult an experienced practitioner.

When even unaware people enter my home they often say how nice it feels. My home is regularly saged and the angels are always invited. It's another beginning to "having a nice day."

4.

To Have or Have Not

Have you ever been ill? Do you know someone who has an illness? What do they have? We have all said and we have all answered these questions. What do they have in common? Think about it.

In Chapter One we talked about our thoughts creating energy patterns. We also displayed the power of our minds and the mixed messages we have sent the universe and God. Those mixed messages diffuse our intention. They also weaken our power.

Now, does anyone want to be ill? Sometimes the

answer is yes. We've all known someone who wanted a little sympathy. Being sick is one way to get it. But, wait. Did that someone really want sympathy? Perhaps they just wanted attention or love. It is my belief that events happen for us, not to us. Let me repeat that: it is my belief that events happen for us, not to us. This is so important I could repeat it for the next ten pages. In business we used to say, "there are no problems, only opportunities." Guess what: what is good business, is also good for us personally. That's right - even sickness happens for us! Of course, no one really wants to be ill. Then why do we take possession of the illness? Most of you probably answered yes to the first three questions at the start of this chapter. Yes, you have been ill. Yes, you know someone who has been ill. Yes, you've said they have_____(ailment), or I have _____(illness).

Is a message beginning to ring in your ears? The next step in "having a nice day" is to be aware of what you take possession. If you don't want it, don't take possession of it. By saying we <u>have</u> it, that's exactly what we are doing. This is discipline. It works, and it is work. We all know every journey begins with a first step. You've already been cleansed of Spiritual Attachments. Now, we must begin within.

Gary Schineller

So, what do you say? We can't remain speechless, can we? Here are a few suggestions: "You may have been *diagnosed* with a condition," or "You may be *fighting* or *suffering* from an ailment," but please do not have it. Unless, you want it.

Perhaps this point might resonate more clearly with this example. Consider someone who says, "I have a cold." Then they pray to be well or wish they were well. My gosh what does God and the universe think you want: to have or have not? Answer the question and don't fib! Remember, for some a condition or ailment is desirable. That's okay. Just be aware that it is your choice. Earlier I said this was work. It is. And the benefits are better than any 401K you've ever considered.

Another signal to release a condition is the word "my." How many times have we said: my problem, my disease, my sickness, etc? Quite a few, I'm sure.

Once again, unless you want the condition, do not tell the universe or God that you want it, by taking possession of it. We've demonstrated how powerful we are, and medical science has proven it. We don't have to understand it. The choice to be happy, healthy, and successful is ours!

Every client I have worked with, regardless of the condition, has embraced this. Today they are all healed. Those conditions include medical diagnoses of HIV, cancer, migraines, arthritis, infectious conditions, Chronic Fatigue Syndrome, allergies, asthma and many more. Each healing process begins with releasing the condition. Many of you have heard that before, and your reply was a half-hearted: "Oh yeah, sure I release it, but I still have it!" Now, you have a method to release it. A discipline. Suddenly, your messages and your intention will start to become consistent. Your power is growing, even at this very moment.

What happens when we slip? Let's say we're in conversation and someone hears you cough or sneeze. And they simply ask: "Do you have a cold?" You answer "Yes." It's all right. We all slip. It just becomes less and less the more you are aware, the more you work at it.

To help on this path here are some examples:

I have a cold.	cancel, cancel,	I am fighting a cold.
	or	
I have a headache.	cancel, cancel,	I am fighting a headache.
	or	
I have arthritis.	cancel, cancel,	I have been diagnosed with arthritis.
	or	

Gary Schineller

I am trying.	cancel, cancel,	I am working.
	or	
I am sorry.	cancel, cancel,	I apologize.
	or	
I am afraid.	cancel, cancel,	I am perfect. There is never any thing to be afraid of.
	or	
I am mad.	cancel, cancel,	I am loving and grateful for this experience.
	or	
I have a toothache.	cancel, cancel,	I am experienc ing toothache pain.

Toothache pain was actually a turning point in my life! I'll explain.

About ten years ago, I was regularly attending a spiritual development class. At this particular time I was also planning a trip to Europe and was going to miss a week's class. When I announced this to the group we decided that while in Europe, at the day and time the group was meeting, I would find a quiet place and meditate. I was to send the group a one-word message. Just before leaving I also had a dental appointment. The dentist was to fill a cavity. While doing so, he said the one word you never want to hear your dentist say: "Oops!" It seems while drilling he had punctured the pulp chamber of my tooth. He decided to place a temporary filling in it. If it gave me a problem, I would need a root canal. I left for my trip, and meditated at the appropriate time. All was very well until I arrived home. It seems the air pressure changes of the flight triggered one whale of a toothache. The pain was intense with swelling to match. As luck would have it, my dentist wasn't able to see me until the next day. (Remember there are no coincidences.) That afternoon I labored over whether to attend my class. I decided to go. Even if the pain was too intense to meditate, at least I would find out if my message was received.

To my delight, my one word message was received and written on paper! The word was "Love." Plus they had accurately described the room I was in and the topography surrounding me. As a bonus the teacher, Dorothy, offered me healing. She placed a hand on my jaw and prayed. The next day I awoke without pain or swelling. I went to the dentist, who after examining, concluded the tooth was fine and inserted a permanent filling. Dorothy became my favorite dentist and, subsequently, became one of my Reiki teachers. While I have experienced some dental pain, I have not had a filling since then. I am now my favorite dentist. I do not "have" toothaches.

Here's another question? Did my dentist's accident happen to me or for me? Have you ever been financially challenged? If that has ever been your reality, what might you say to the telephone charity solicitor? Previously, you might have said:

> I don't "have" any money! "Cancel, cancel" I am not considering any donations at this time, thank you.

Which would you like the universe to hear?

One of my neighbors, a truly beautiful, retired woman, had been diagnosed with cancer. From the first moment of diagnosis she did not want to relate to being a cancer patient. Her spirit is strong. Her faith is even stronger. Today, she does not "have" cancer. She never took possession of it.

A very powerful obstacle which presents itself to a lot of us is worry. And it's a biggee! The National Mental Health Committee reports that half of all the people in America's hospital beds are constant worriers. Do you suppose they say, "I am worried?" Mental distress can lead to migraine headaches, arthritis, heart trouble, cystitis, colitis, headaches, ulcers, depression, digestive disorders and, yes, even death. Add to that list the mental fatigue of nights without sleep and days without peace and then we get a glimpse of the havoc worry plays in destroying the quality and quantity of life.

This story tells it all: The Power of Worrying. Death was walking toward a city one morning and a man asked, "What are you going to do?" "I'm going to take 100 people," Death said. "That's horrible," the man said. "That's the way it is," Death said. "That's what I do." The man hurried to warn everyone he could about Death's plan. As evening fell, he met Death again. "You told me you were going to take 100 people," the man said. "Why did 1,000 die?" "I kept my word," Death responded. "I only took 100 people. Worry took the others."

Worry is a fatal disease of the heart, for its beginning signals the end of faith. Do you remember what the Desiderata says? "Nurture strength of spirit to shield you in sudden misfortune. But do not distress yourself with dark imaginings. Many fears are born of fatigue and lone-liness." And "no doubt the universe is unfolding as it should." You can see the importance of faith in releasing worry. Further, to that end I suggest you release the regrets

Gary Schineller

of yesterday, refuse the fears of tomorrow and receive instead the peace of today. It's yet another step in "How to: Have a Nice Day."

Wouldn't this entire process be easier if everyone were well? Of course it would be. And of course we'd like everyone to be well. Here's something you can do to help. If you are a commercial or public service announcement writer, please adopt the information from this chapter. Please do not have spokespeople say things like I "have" cystic fybrosis, I "have" cancer, etc. Please do not write: "Do you 'have' a headache?" After all, the overriding goal of the pharmaceutical industry and the medical profession is wellness, isn't it? There are many wonderful products which provide relief. And everyone has the right to choose their method of treatment. Please however, do not promote the illness. Please do not ask us to take possession of illness.

If you are not in these industries, but know someone who is, kindly pass this information along. I believe in the human spirit. I believe we all really want everyone to be well. The simplicity of this information and its power is yours for the using. It is "How to: Have a Nice Day!"

Earlier, we said this was work; it is. And the benefits

are greater than any wage you have ever earned. Here's a short story which might help make the point.

Jane was a devout, church going woman. Only, it appeared to her that her life was falling apart. So she prayed and she prayed that God would help her win the lottery. Then she lost her job. She prayed some more. Then she lost her car. She prayed some more. When she was about to lose her house she cried as she prayed to God. "Why have you forsaken me, God? I've been good. I go to church. All I've asked for is that you help me win the lottery!" This time she heard God's voice as He said: "Would you at least buy a ticket?"

You've bought the book. If you do the work, you will have a nice day.

5.

Humor or a Sound Can be worth a 1000 Pills

❦

One of my favorite Reverend friends and his wife had decided on Saturday that they were due to commune with nature. They decided they'd go horseback riding. Now, he had never been riding before, so guess what happened? Twice, he got thrown. Then he gave up. It's now Saturday evening. They are back home and he's working on his sermon. He decides he should find the spiritual message in why he fell off. That would be the topic of his sermon. After all, he believed that this did not happen to him, but for him. So, he meditates, and meditates and meditates. In fact, he's up till 3 AM working on his sermon. Understandably, he oversleeps and so does his wife. This means he doesn't have time to rehearse his sermon with her. That was his normal pattern. And now, because they're late, his wife says she's not going because she doesn't have enough time to get ready. On his way to church, speeding and unrehearsed, our reverend decides to scrap entirely the sermon he was up till 3 AM writing. Instead he's going to speak from his heart. His topic is going to be "sex."

It's now the next day and our Rev's wife is in the supermarket when she runs into one of the parishioners. This parishioner begins to compliment her husband's sermon from the day before. The parishioner went on to say how the Pastor also seemed to know everything about his topic. To which the wife replied: "I don't know how. He only tried it twice and got thrown off both times!"

Why am I telling you a joke? Well, for the same reason I begin every class, every meeting, and every healing session with humor. Laughter has been proven, by a Harvard experiment, to open the Chakras. The Chakras are energy centers of the body. (See the chart on page 70) They transmit energy when you are healthy. They don't when you are not or, more importantly, when you are about to experience illness.

I, too, have proven the effect of laughter on closed or non-vibrant Chakras. There are three types of laughter:

Ho Ho Ho (Santa's deep belly laugh)

Ha Ha Ha (normal or midrange laughter)

He He He (high pitched laughter)

The deep laughter will open Chakras one and two. The midrange laughter will open Chakras three and four, while the high pitched laughter will open five, six, and seven. Each type of laughter should be hearty.

You can read Chakras with your hands. Find a quiet place with a friend. Rub your palms together several times. Stand on the left side of your friend and place the palm of your left hand about one to two inches over or in front of the seven areas highlighted on the chart. Slowly, move them off those areas. Do you feel the difference in heat/energy? For perfectly balanced health the heat/energy should be the same over all Chakras. If there's an imbalance or a blockage, employ the laughter technique for one to two minutes. Then take another reading. You've heard laughter is the best medicine. Now you've proved it. How many times after a belly laugh have you said: "That felt good?"

The Body's Seven Main Energy Centers

#7 CROWN CHAKRA
Location: Top of Head   Color: Violet or White

#6 BROW CHAKRA
(Third Eye)
Location: Center of
Forehead
Color: Indigo

#5 THROAT CHAKRA
Location: Throat Area
Color: Sky Blue

#4 HEART CHAKRA
Location: Center
of Chest
Color: Green or
Pink

#3 SOLAR PLEXUS CHAKRA
Location:
Above the
Navel, below
the Waist
Color: Yellow

#2 NAVEL CHAKRA
(Sacral Plexus)
Location: Navel Area
Color: Orange

#1 ROOT CHAKRA
(Base Chakra)
Location: Base of Spine
Color: Red or Black

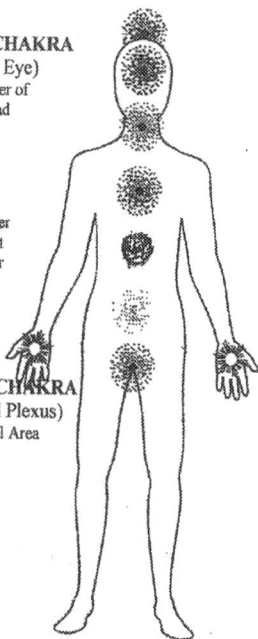

There are also powerful energy centers in the palm of each hand and on the sole of each foot.

Gary Schineller

There's another method of reading Chakras which will provide a visual picture. You can use a necklace with an evenly balanced pendant on it or buy a pendulum from your favorite store that perhaps sold you the sage. I prefer a pendulum with a long cord, as well as one which separates or unscrews. If you select this type, unscrew it before each use and blow inside the threaded area. This will release any residual energy. Then, without imparting motion from your hand, hang the pendulum on top or in front of each Chakra. Again, do this while standing on the left side of your friend. The energy coming from each Chakra will cause the pendulum to swing. The wider the amplitude the healthier the Chakra. If there is weakness, employ laughter as we have just described and measure it again.

But, what have you just accomplished by regaining balanced energy flow? Just like priming a pump, the body now has a chance to continue that flow. However, some ailments or conditions also have a rather strong presence and will require repetitive treatment. After all, a prescription normally does not consist of one pill, does it?

Now, since most of us don't want to be seen as laughing fools, let me recommend some additional means of opening your Chakras. Please, however, remember to keep the benefits of laughter as part of your daily life. Also, please do not make your humor at the expense of someone else. Your healing should never be at the cost of someone else's well being. Ultimately, it will not help you either.

For those of you gifted with musical talent, I also recommend song. Consider the types of laughter or the vocal ranges of laughter. The same concept applies to the notes of the scale. "So sing, sing a song. Don't worry that it's not good enough for anyone else to hear. Just sing, sing a song." (words & music by Joe Raposo: Sesame Street) Sound familiar? Our lessons are all around us, if we just pay attention. What feels good usually is good for you. When did you ever feel poorly after or while singing?

There's also an interesting bit of history attached to this. Most religious services employ song. Many begin and end with song. And don't you normally feel good after attending a service. Is this a coincidence? I don't think so!

Consider your favorite musical artists. Who are they? What ranges do their voices possess? In my lifetime the most popular singers were largely those that possessed a high range. From Enrico Caruso to Michael Jackson,

Gary Schineller

Mario Lanza to the Righteous Brothers, Frank Sinatra to the Beatles, Crosby, Stills, Nash and Young to Minnie Ripperton, Janis Joplin to Sara Brightman, Pavoratti to Madonna, and so on, and so on. Sure, there are exceptions, but for the most part contemporary societies always seem to have applauded the high ranges. And what Chakra is associated with high notes? That's right, the Crown Chakra. The Crown Chakra is also known by many as our Spiritual connection. And what does our society tend to do with celebrities? They are practically worshiped. I wonder where that came from? Isn't it interesting that there is often a physical and/or Spiritual root to our feelings? So remember, sing a song: La la, la la la la, la la, la la la la, la la la, la la la la!

The Chakra Chart also lists colors. We know from physics that all things have vibration. Yes, each color possesses a separate and distinct vibration. The colors listed on the chart match the vibration of the corresponding Chakra. Therefore, the wearing of these colors can stimulate Chakra vibration. For example if the Throat Chakra is weak, you might wear a scarf that is sky blue. It's important to note that the symptoms of a condition might have nothing to do with the location of the weakened Chakra. For example I've found someone experiencing migraine headaches to have a weakened Navel Chakra. Of course he needed to wear an orange shirt.

The final means of opening your Chakras employs the use of hands-on healing or Reiki. Reiki is defined as universal life force energy. It is Spiritually based and energy driven. If you choose to explore this I recommend you seek out a certified Reiki Master. Some non-denominational and non-proselytizing churches can provide a list of practitioners for you.

These are all ways of priming the Chakra energy pumps. They do not represent treatment for the cause of ailments or conditions. In most cases this type of healing gives enough relief for the body to do what it was designed to do - be healthy. However, it is my experience that symptoms may return if the underlying life lesson has not been learned. The Pleadians are known for a phrase which I use often: "When the (stuff) is about to hit the fan, say goody, goody here it comes." This is just another way of saying "events happen for us, not to us." They are our opportunities to grow. They represent yet another opportunity to: "Have a Nice Day."

6.

Thought Word and Deed

——◆——

At the outset everyone has an impression of what this chapter is about. The obvious is: think good thoughts; say nice words; and do good deeds. You're right. But perhaps you've never connected the rest of the story, the why, the how and the courage to stay above the line or to stay in the light. It's easy when all is going well, but can we do it during those dark, difficult, challenging days? Yes, we can!

It's time I shared a warning. Living this work or raising our vibration does not mean that we will cease to be challenged. On the contrary. We may experience more challenges, more tests than ever before. Remember the laws of Physics discussed in Chapter One. Patterns are like a "body in motion. It will tend to stay in motion until acted upon by an equal or greater force." Then why should we continue this work, you might ask. The difference is this. Before doing this work, you still experienced many challenges, didn't you? You just may not have recognized them. You may have just anguished or worried about why things weren't going right.

While doing this work we become more aware of the true nature of our challenges. We will begin to see, to incorporate into our daily consciousness, the reality that these events indeed do happen *for* us, not to us. With that knowledge, as part of our daily consciousness, we will live its true benefits. Let's start with some simple examples of "Thought, Word and Deed" in action to raise this power, to continue to raise our vibration. For those of us who have attended college this would be the 101 level.

Do you jog or walk for exercise? I do. When jogging do you pass by others? Do they react? Do you? Is there any exchange? Perhaps you've had an experience like mine.

I live in a country club community where every morning we have a large assortment of walkers, joggers, bicyclists, and skaters. Being in Florida, there's also a percentage of transients. What a shame that within this idyllic and peaceful setting almost no one greeted each other. Instead, they simply looked down or attempted to ignore each other. Then I moved in! And I'm happy to report that after about a week of "Good Mornings" and pleasant small talk, everyone now smiles and greets their neighbors. Of course, the transients still have to be taught, but they learn very quickly, courtesy of our collective consciousness. Think about the alternatives. Since this was also happening for me versus to me some might say the day that changed the world, "Hello, From My Heart" Day was actually born right here.

Remember, everyone has a choice. Suppose someone is visibly attempting to ignore you. What do you do? Mentally, you might think something negative about that person, perhaps internally call them a name, perhaps even out loud. It's sometimes very tempting, especially, after you've extended a warm, smiling greeting.

We've all experienced this. Yet, now think about the choice you have the next time, even though the next time they might continue to ignore you! All that really matters is how you internalize it, because, how you think about it is who you are. That's right. The way you think about someone else, or what you think about someone else is a reflection of yourself. Do you buy that? I hope so. You'll want to keep this in mind for an exercise we're going to do in a short while.

Now, let's jump to the 102 level of this thought. Let's expand our good wishes, our good mornings, and our waves to include complimentary commentary. That's right, find something to compliment the occasional passer-by. It might be a hat, an outfit, their pace or anything at all. What happens? You guessed it. This task is so simple, but the rewards are so great. And you can apply this to any interactive aspect of your life.

I'll stick with jogging for one moment longer. One of those lady walkers I described earlier wears a hat. She seems to have a rather unique style of hats, which I find pleasant. I must admit I believe she originally used her hat to hide a little. And I don't mean just from the sun. The brim is a cap style, which seemed to aid her intent of looking down and straight ahead. At first she tried to ignore my "good morning" greeting. However, after several days her

Gary Schineller

natural sense of politeness took over, and I got a smile. Then I received a "good morning." The next day I said: "How's my favorite hat lady?" Do you know how you feel when someone's looking forward to seeing you? Well, that's the way I feel whenever I now see my new favorite hat lady.

Today, I live in a very friendly neighborhood. Almost everyone greets each other when passing by foot or by car. In some cases it's almost like a contest now, to see who can wave or smile first. I like where I live. I always do. I'm reminded of a favorite TV show, Cheers. This was and is one of the most popular shows ever on TV. It's the place "where everybody knows you name!" And most of the TV viewing public did. The same feeling of that song can be yours, and you don't have to go to a bar to get it. For me it's another great beginning of a very nice day

We're going to take this one giant step further in the Chapter entitled "Hello, From My Heart." This describes a scientifically proven exercise which demonstrated…how we can and are changing the world.

Now, let's look at an example of this same process in business. Of course, you already greet everyone in the office. But, how about when you answer the telephone?

The next time the phone rings, smile before you pick it up and continue to smile during your greeting. Those calling will have a nice feeling and be glad they called. It's what we call a no-lose proposition. Regardless of your business, it will be better.

And how about "that" person at the office. You know the one I mean. They come in both sexes, and are typified by negativity. Sometimes they are mean, sometimes critical, gossipy, backstabbing, etc. Got the picture? I know you do.

Well, how have you dealt with these situations before? A lot of us "tried" to ignore them. And what happened? First of all we were "trying." What happens when we "try?" Remember Chapter 1? Instead let's look at the proactive posture. Yes, initiate a "good morning." Find different things about that person to compliment. And be sincere. In addition, remember the power of your thoughts. Do you remember my pool-shooting story or my "pretty sissy" story? I was able to cause someone to miss the easiest pool shot just by focusing a concentrated thought. And my "pretty sissy" was able to stay in 53 degree Fahrenheit water for thirty minutes. If we focus on positive energy toward "that" person, what do you think you will achieve? Here's a tip. You don't even have to be in the same room. If you've been practicing the principles we have discussed so far you'll be amazed how quick you'll notice positive change. Your power is getting stronger.

Consider the past. When we attempt to ignore an individual we usually "have" thoughts of fear, worry, or anger. If we "have" those thoughts what are we promoting? That's right. Now, we can make it a nice day!

OK, you've had the undergraduate 101 and 102 work. It's time for some graduate work. The following is an exercise you will most certainly enjoy. In fact you will probably first learn this exercise and then share it with your friends and loved ones. Also, if you're beginning a relationship, it's a terrific way to get to know someone.

To get started, tear some paper into eight small pieces about 2" x 3" each. You'll also need something to write with. Here we go.

Imagine you are planning a dinner party and you're going to invite six guests. However, this is a very special dinner party. For this party your guest list can include people from all of time. That's right, you can invite people from the ages, people you know, or people you don't know.

This is your ideal dinner party. There's only one catch. One person has to be someone you don't particularly care for or really don't like. Please put one name on each of six pieces of paper. (Kindly do this now before reading further.) You will have two pieces of paper left over.

Gary Schineller

Great, now imagine it's the day of your party. Dinner is in the oven. You've really outdone yourself. It's going to be a very special evening. You've even hired someone to serve. At this time, some of your guests have already arrived when there's a knock on your door. To your surprise there are two additional people at the door. They were not invited and did not necessarily come together. However, they can tell that you are about to have a party, and because you are so polite, you invite them in. One of them you like very much, while the other you don't particularly care for, or just plain don't like. Please write each of their names on your remaining two pieces of paper.

Now, on the back of each piece of paper I want you to write the first adjective, or descriptive word which pops into your head about that particular person. This should take a maximum of thirty seconds. Begin now.

OK, now all of your guests have arrived. Suddenly, your telephone rings. As surprising as this is, you are being unavoidably called away from your own party. You explain this to your guests with the hope that you might be able to return later in the evening. However, dinner is ready and you do have someone there to serve. To insure that everyone has a good time you are now going to arrange place cards for the seating arrangement. (Please clear a suitable space on your bed, desk, or table and do this now. Please do not read ahead until you have done this. You will waste the benefits of this exercise if you do.) Please set your table.

Great. Your table is set. Please put all the names face down. Do you know what you're looking at? You are looking at a picture of yourself. That's right. The basic tenet of Gestalt psychology is this: "What you see in someone else is a reflection of yourself." If you think about it, it makes sense. If it wasn't something you could personally relate to, it would be meaningless, right? Here's an example.: Have you ever witnessed behavior you simply could not under-stand? How about the shootings at Columbine? That's the good news! You can't understand it. You can't relate to it. Thank God, it's not part of your personality.

Now, let's get back to your table. First, what is its shape? Is it rectangular or circular? If it's rectangular, does it have seating at the ends? The shape of your table tends to indicate how you view life. Do you view life as a whole (circular or oval shape), or do you view life more dualisti-cally (rectangular)? If you have placed someone at the heads of your table you have given them power. If you have placed someone you don't like at both of the heads of your table, you have given that which you don't like great power.

Now look at where you have placed those you don't particularly care for. Are they next to each other or sepa-rated? There is a relationship between all elements of your-self. Typically, if you isolate that which you don't care for, you deal with it with the personality trait sitting next to it. Try this for visualization. Take the pieces sitting on either side of what you don't like and place them over half of that piece. When you are perceived by others to be what you don't like - or - you get caught, these are the personality elements you will use to move out of, or get you out of that state. If your "don't likes" are seated next to each other they typically feed each other, but also have less power because you are only using two elements to cover them up.

What you are left with after all the covering up is who you really are. It's the person you enjoy being when you don't have to deal with anything else.

Well, how do you like yourself? One final caveat: the purpose of this exercise is not to create a new breed of psychoanalysts. This has been a very general interpretation. Aberrations may exist due to factors of environment. Critical interpretations should only be formed in the presence of a professional.

You might like to save your pieces of the "Parts Party" in your journal. Then in six months or a year perform this exercise again. Do you think there will be a difference? Yes, there will! I promise.

The purpose of this exercise is to demonstrate once again the power of your thoughts. Remember, what you see in someone else is a reflection of yourself. Therefore, discipline is called for when you act or react to someone else. If you choose a path of action, not reaction, you will have a nice day, every day!

Let me be more specific. When you think non-desirable or unpleasant thoughts about someone, you are really therefore, thinking that about yourself. That's right. If you call someone a name, consider now that you are actually referring to a part of yourself. This has been popularly reduced to this example. Take your right hand and point your index finger at someone. Notice, that as we point one finger at someone else, three are pointing back at us. We have all been guilty of talking about someone else or calling them a name. Maybe next time, there won't be a next time!

We have all heard that to be healthy and happy we need to love ourselves. We've heard the lesson that you can't love someone else until you love yourself. Well, now are we really loving ourselves when we call someone else a name or even think it? Aha!

Here's some additional motivation. When you hear someone else talking about someone, we call this gossip, and it usually involves some kind of name calling. Give yourself a wink, because you've just learned something about the person who is gossiping! Haven't you? Now, consider that this knowledge is becoming widespread. Will you ever gossip again?

In the spiritual realm, all faiths of which I am aware teach that we should not be judgmental. We've probably all heard, "Judgement is mine, sayeth the Lord." Isn't it interesting? Modern Psychology is teaching us today what was written thousands of years ago! Everything old is new again!

Some of you might now be saying, "Yeah, yeah that's fine in church, but I can't apply that to business. I'll get killed!" Let me say this unto you: The more you practice these disciplines the more powerful you will become.

The more we practice, the more we work at this, the more we will see and experience positive results. The more we love ourselves, the more we are able to love others, and truly Have a Nice Day. We'll prove this later in the Chapter "Hello, From My Heart."

Remember the *Desiderata*? "Exercise caution in your business affairs; for the world is full of trickery...." Here's an example of trickery and how this discipline worked in my life. Most of my career I have spent in broadcasting. Today, I still do some consulting. As I was negotiating a recent contract (the network shall remain nameless), I noticed that when the paperwork arrived the terms were different from what we had negotiated. Now, as you might expect I keep copious notes and knew the error was my client's, and obviously in his favor. When I presented the discrepancy, he became rather heated and it appeared the contract might go south. Therefore, I assumed a posture of "The customer is always right," the first time. However, my antennae were now raised that this might be a personality trait and could resurface in another form later. Hard copies (dated and signed) were kept of everything. Sure enough, when it came time to get paid for the final stage of my contract, there was a problem. To make matters worse, the CEO and founder of this innovative network was the brother of the V.P. of Marketing. My contract had been negotiated with the V.P. of Marketing. You might expect that the CEO is going to believe his brother before an independent consultant.

Therefore, in my summation, which provided full documentation, I included this line to the CEO: "Your brother loves you and this is how (saving money) he feels he can best contribute to your idea." I got paid by return mail! And there's more good news. We may continue to do business. I don't think any other pattern of response would have generated this result. Think about it. What if I had called the V.P. a liar and a cheat? Would that have produced the same reply? If I had the CEO would have perhaps reacted defensively of his brother and accused me of the misdeed. In a sense he would have felt that what I was saying was a reflection of myself? So the next time you hear someone calling someone else a name, think about it. Is that what they think about themselves? Most importantly, how do you want others to think about you; and how do you want to feel about yourself? I love you! I think you are perfect!

When you stay in this light - and it is work - you are raising your vibration. When we raise our vibration to a higher pitch, we become and our thoughts become that much more powerful. Spiritually speaking, we are getting closer to being one with the Father, truly in His image. You're getting back to the Garden. And there is nothing more powerful than that.

Many of you have been in services or meetings where there's a part when you are asked to hug your neighbor. In my meetings, I add something to that. I ask everyone to first look each other in the eye, and say "I love you" Then we hug. For those of us that sense or feel energy, imagine the vibration which now grows in the room. It's very powerful. Do it! And it doesn't matter if you know the person or not. Just do it.

Another example of the power of our thoughts and words can be found in the person who, when beginning a particular task, says "This is going to drive me crazy!" Now that we have graduated past our 102 level, what do you think their experience is going to be? What are they affirming? Is it likely that they will get what they are asking for? Simply put, yes.

We have the opportunity to choose our intention during every moment. When more of us choose a positive, eager, and upbeat attitude it will spread. It's our choice. It's also our responsibility - to ourselves, to our company, our country and our planet.

Well, we've covered "Thought" and "Word." What about "Deeds?" Yes, we're all going to become Boy Scouts or Girl Scouts. Except, we're not just going to do one good deed a day and we don't have to wear a uniform. There's also no saluting involved. Unless, of course, you just can't resist.

Many of us do good deeds all the time. Great. Keep it up. I bet we can do more. A good deed, however, needs to be treated like a gift. In the Jewish faith it's called a Mitzvah. It's the kind of gift we give when we don't expect one in return. Now that's the hard part. We can never ever say or think, well I did this for you; why won't you do that for me. Then the gift becomes a loan, or a job from which you expect a return or compensation. This is a great opportunity to get creative. Here's an idea.

Two of my neighbors are older and retired. They also subscribe to a daily newspaper, which is normally tossed near the curb. Since I'm an early riser, I'm always the first to retrieve my paper. As I do, I also retrieve each of theirs and place it standing up or leaning on the wall next to their door. Wouldn't you like to have your paper delivered like this? Remember, they are older. This way, they don't even have to bend all the way down to pick it up.

The best part of this was doing it undetected. It took almost a year before I was found out. And the way I was found out was kind of special. Another of my neighbors from across the way had apparently spied my act, and one day said to one of my neighbors, "Boy I wish I lived next to

GARY SCHINELLER

Gary!" Isn't that nice?

Are you having a nice day yet? It's fun to get sneaky, playful, and at the same time help others to have a nice day. In the process, guess what? You are creating a nice day for yourself. It is often said, that as we give we receive. It's another way to Have a Nice Day.

7.

Invite an Angel to Lunch

—◆—

*Y*es, I'm serious. Invite an angel or a bunch of them to lunch, to drive with, to play with, to work with, or any old time. If you do, they will come. I promise. They love to be invited. They also love us without condition or judgment.

Here are some examples from my life.

I've noticed that drivers in every locale seem to have their own culture. In Florida they love to tailgate, regardless of speed. Now, we know that can be very dangerous. So, what can we do? We could make hand gestures to the car in back of us. We could speed to such a high rate that they can't keep up. We could pull over and let them pass and maybe you've got some other alternatives. Judging by the ever increasing prevalence of "Road Rage" we could use a few. Here's what I do: First, I say, either out loud or silently, "I AM protected." "I AM protected." (Remember, Chapter 1?) Then, I call upon the angels (again out loud or silently) to join me for my Highest and Best. After that I request that they suggest to the driver who is tailgating that he would be more comfortable and safe at a greater distance. I repeat this several times and then look in my rearview mirror. Ninety percent of the time I am delighted at what I see. Statistically, this is what we call success.

Okay then, what about the other 10% of the time? Then, I acknowledge that I am in the perfect place at the perfect time. Even if the other vehicle is still there, it is at least not causing me stress. After all, I AM protected. The next most important thing is to thank the angels. They like to be thanked. Wouldn't you?

One evening several years ago I was driving to a waterfront club where a rhythm and blues band was to be playing. I was driving alone. While driving I decided to suggest

Gary Schineller

to the angels that it would be very nice to meet a lady with whom I could enjoy a spiritual conversation. And it wouldn't hurt if she was beautiful and loved to dance! Don't jump to conclusions now, I think you'll be surprised at what happened.

I arrived and found there were no seats available near my two friends, so I sat alone at the crowded bar. In a short while two women walked in. One was absolutely stunning, although she was about fifteen years younger than I. You might say she's the type of lady who when she walked in the room everyone's head turned. Got the picture?

Then she and her girlfriend began to dance. You guessed it. She was a terrific dancer. Expectedly, when she returned to the bar every single fella in the place was negotiating for her attention. I could not have been more surprised when, after she received a drink, she came over to talk to me! Remember, you're still going to be surprised with the ending. But, this part you guessed. After a short while our conversation turned to spirituality. She was wonderfully well-versed and fascinating. After we danced, we went outside to the docks and continued our conversation. So, you might imagine, I was very, very happy with the angels. As we continued our conversation, I learned she was visiting her girlfriend who had just gotten divorced. She was from North Carolina - and so was her husband!

The moral to the story: when making a request of the angels, be very specific. They have quite a sense of humor.

Is this the end of that story? It could be. But let's reflect on something we said in the introduction, "Events happen for us, not to us." Why did the angels give me this situation? Sure, it's playful. But, remember what we also said about tests and how we are given the same test or challenge over and over until it is no longer a challenge?

What would have happened if I had pursued a relationship with this married lady? At best her marriage would have been compromised. And, I would have broken the Golden Rule. Every faith throughout the planet has a version of this "do unto others as you would have them do unto you" principle. I am committed to it. My commitment was tested. I passed. When we see the totality of our experiences we really are having a nice day. Thank you, angels.

Here's an easy way for us to enjoy our angels. The next time you are driving to a mall or someplace else where you will have to employ public parking, ask your angels to please provide you the perfect parking place. Your friends will be amazed at how often you are blessed with a space right in front of, or very near the door.

Have you ever thought you lost or misplaced something? Of course, we all have. Well, the next time ask your angels to help you find it. You'll be amazed. I have many examples. Recently, I thought I had lost a crystal on a gold chain. I asked for help and was guided to check behind the headboard of my bed. First, I looked over the top from the middle and then to the left.

As I wedged my head between the lamp and the bed post, still looking behind the frame, there it was; six inches from my nose, hanging on the bed post. I told you they have a sense of humor.

Do you shoot golf or play any other sports? Invite the angels. You'll be glad you did, I promise.

Several years ago I was leaving to teach a Reiki class. Earlier that day I had noticed that the temperature gauge on my car was reading just below hot, so before I left I attempted to pop the hood and add water. Only, the hood would not open. Now, I couldn't be late for class. So, I asked the angels to join me and help me to safely get to class. Immediately, the gauge began to rise toward hot. The trip was twenty-six miles over country and city roads. I made every light and arrived on time while constantly praying for the angels to be with me. The class was in one of my student's homes. After class we went outside. Their cat was on the roof of my car meowing to the sky. They had never seen their cat do that before or since. I leave it to your imagination to determine what was going on. However, the hood would still not open.

Yet, I made the trip, and again made every light. The next morning my hood was already ajar when I went outside. The radiator was almost empty. And, my faith was soaring with gratitude.

Angels will make their presence known in any number of ways. One is the brushing of the hair on your arms and legs. This can have a rather tickle like feeling. A very magical moment in my life was my ordination. During the ceremony, the angels were so happy that uncontrollably, right in the middle of the ceremony, I broke into the most joyous laughter. You know, the kind that comes from your heart. It starts with a smile that gets broader and broader until it just plain erupts. The angels were truly present. And their present was this wonderful laughter. Every One joined. Every One laughed. Every One had a really nice day.

At this time a short discussion on faith is in order. Earlier I shared the definition of an atheist. He is someone without invisible means of support. Personally, my faith in God is supported by consistently repeating examples of His "presents." It is not of one faith, but of all. I celebrate our Oneness with the Father and each other.

Have you ever associated a particular song with someone who has crossed over? Have you noticed that particular song might come on the radio at a very appropriate time? That is their angelic way of sending you love. Some would call this a "coincidink." I don't. Are you having a nice day yet?

Are you distanced from a loved one? Would you like to send them an angelic message? As you retire, picture your loved one in your mind and ask the angels to deliver your message. Do this for several evenings. Then, call your loved one. You'll probably be greeted with something like; "I've been thinking about you," or "You know, you've been on my mind lately." Thank you, angels.

Do you use an alarm clock to wake you? For most of

my life I have not. Here's a simple experiment. When you retire, ask your angels to give you a restful sleep and to please wake you thirty minutes earlier than your alarm setting. State the exact time you would like to be awakened. Surprise, it works!

Do you dream? Keep a journal next to your bed. When you awaken write down every detail you can remember. Include all the colors of everything you see. Our angels send us many messages in our dreams. Their interpretation is often very simple. I recommend consulting a knowledgable practitioner or finding the book about dream interpretation which feels like it is the right one for you. Normally, it is the first one you either pick up or focus on in the book store. Pleasant dreams, indeed! You'll also find it fascinating to go back in your journal and read what you dreamt about a month, a year ago, etc.

Have you noticed that you think you're seeing something out of the corner of your eye, yet as you turn, there is nothing there? No, you don't need your eyes checked. We are all experiencing this more and more. As our vibration or consciousness increases - and remember everyone's is - we are getting glimpses of alternate dimensions. Usually, what you are seeing is shadow-like in form. Say "hi" to your

Gary Schineller

angels. They love us.

If you are blessed to have a newly-born child in your life, you're going to love this experience. While holding the baby, call upon all the angels to bring their light and love. Now, watch the baby's eyes as they grow brighter and wider. Most also smile. Most newly-born children can still see them. Do you think you'll be helping your baby to Have a Nice Day?

Many of us have had life saving or injury saving experiences which defy any logical interpretation. Perhaps now, you have an answer. If you feel drawn to explore this further there are guided meditations through which you can meet your Guardian Angel. You might also avail yourself of a reputable "Spiritual-Intuitive-Counselor." In addition to family members you could be surprised, as I was, with who is watching out for you.

There are thousands and thousands of angels. They love to be called upon.

One pastor I know, Rev. Donna Jeanne refers to there being a giant unemployment line of angels. Use them. They know only how to love us. You'll be glad you did, and you'll be continuing to Have a Nice Day!

8.

Good News

— ◦ —

*O*ur Vibrations are all being raised. Even our beloved planet Earth is vibrating at a rate higher than ever in our recorded history.

As Earth rotates on its axis, it also vibrates. This is measured at the North Pole. When measurements were first being taken the vibration was in inches. Now, it's in kilometers. Planes use gyroscopes. They used to be required to receive annual calibration. Now, I understand that monthly calibration is required.

In Chapter Two, we talked about the Tower of Babel

and how man used to have full use of his brain. The good news is that as the planet vibrates, and all of us increase our vibrations, this is being returned. While every one is experiencing this, it is my belief that those on a spiritual quest are receiving more of these gifts. In other words, everyone reading this book is enjoying more of these gifts. Now, this increased usage of our brain has nothing to do with intelligence quotients. The first example that everyone is enjoying has to do with telepathy.

Have you found that in the past year you have experienced more situations where either you have said something and the other person said, "I was just thinking that," or vice versa? Or, maybe you've experienced finishing more of others' sentences, either out loud or to yourself? This is the beginning of telepathic communications, and everyone I have surveyed finds it to be true. Our experiences frequently are most noticeable with loved ones, but range from business to perfect strangers. If you have not noticed this yet, pay attention. You'll be glad you did.

Imagine what we can accomplish when all of us speak the same language. This applies to all aspects of our lives, including business. Now, that's good news! Most disagreements are born of a lack of understanding. And since every culture believes in their version of the Golden Rule, this is the happiest news of hope any of us could ask for.

For what follows, it's important to know the difference between prayer and meditation. Very simply, prayer is when we talk to God. Meditation is when we listen. Listening can take the forms of knowing, seeing, or hearing. For new students of meditation I am including the following exercise. The point of this exercise is to show you where to look for your messages.

By now it should be clear that I celebrate and honor all forms of spiritual expression. Therefore, endorsement of any particular faith is not intended.

Place this page under a bright light. Concentrate on the 4 dots in the center of the picture for about 30 seconds. Then, close you eyes and tilt your head to the light.

What do you see?

I began meditating in 1969. The first time I heard the voice of God was May 21, 2001. If love was a sound, this was it; pure, sweet love! There was no sexual identity to the sound. And the sound was not audible, but telepathic.

Those beginning meditation today can count on a greatly accelerated timetable for learning and experiencing. All of my students today report experiences after just their first session. As we've said, the vibration is now much higher.

On May 21, 2001, I asked if the information I had received about the Tower of Babel and those gifts being returned was accurate. I was told "Yes." I also asked if this was part of what many have called the ascension. Again, I was told "Yes." Then I wanted to know what we could do to help. This time the answer was only slightly more lengthy. I was told, "You already know that answer." When I confessed that I would appreciate some specific direction, the answer again was simple: "Love!"

Love, of course, means something different to everyone. Ask anyone. You'll see. And, of course there are no wrong answers. However, let's see if this fits. First, we know love should be without condition. In other words, it's not I love you when you do this, or because you do that, or look like

Gary Schineller

that, etc. It's unconditional. And second, it's without judgement. Can we do this? When we truly love someone it's unconditionally without judgement. This also and especially applies to loving ourselves.

Do you say "yes" to yourself? How many times have you had an idea not to do something, and went ahead and did it anyway? Keep smiling. Of course, we all have many times. Were you generally happy with the way your day turned out? As our ability to love ourselves grows, we will learn to say "yes" to ourselves more frequently. The converse to this is commonly called "beating oneself up." This is clearly, not loving our self. It is entirely judgmental. And we've all done it. When we recognize that we are perfect, that all events are happening for us versus to us, a sense of well being begins to take over our consciousness. It is often said that we truly can not love another if we do not love our self first.

Let's go further on this. Just as I said there are no wrong answers, there can likewise be no wrong people. Their truth may not be your truth, but they don't think they are wrong. Let's take a simple example of someone who is significantly overweight. When they put on their best outfit and look in the mirror what do they see? If you have ever been overweight you know the answer. They see someone looking their very best. And so they should. They are loving themselves without condition or judgment. And if we are to love them, it is not up to us to judge them.

The same is true of cultures. There is one culture I am familiar with which honors winning via any means. In business dealings I have had with many from this country I have found them to lie, cheat, and steal. They celebrate and honor each other for their success. Yet, there is much to be found enjoyable in doing business with them. Knowing these traits I am open and communicative with them, and I protect myself accordingly. You simply build some cushion into the price of doing business. They win and so do you, without judgment and with love.

Einstein had a great way not just with physics, but with phrases. He said, "Whoever undertakes to set himself up as a judge of truth and knowledge is shipwrecked by the laughter of the gods."

Within this context, the common concept of forgiveness is useless or not needed. Heretofore, when we sincerely said, "I forgive you," we were really saying this: "Okay, you were wrong, but...I forgive you." That person's action may be wrong by our standards for our lives, but is it our dominion to judge? Judgement is mine, sayeth the Lord. Every individual deserves to be loved. We don't have to

Gary Schineller

adopt their practices. We do have to love them - without condition, without judgement

I can hear the deafening sounds of "Yeah but," so let's deal with a few. Let's say your mother, your brother, or perhaps your significant other thinks you are nuts. And you, naturally, don't agree with them. Are they demeaning or derisive? Or perhaps they just ignore you. If so, have you explained that this is not how you see yourself? This is not how you deserve to be treated. And, have you explained that you don't need them to agree with you, but you do need them to love you unconditionally without judgement. If we have done all of this without success, we now need to make sure we are loving ourselves. Relationships are very powerful, especially family relationships. If we live in or with a non-loving relationship, sooner or later we'll get sick. It creates stress and stress causes illness. Illness takes many forms. They of course include alcohol and drug abuse along with the more popular varieties.

Do I hear the word guilt? This is the most common device used for manipulation within our society. Guilt creates victimhood. It is entirely based in judgement. It is extraordinarily unhealthy and can result in a whole myriad of conditions that can range from being accident-prone to disease to even suicide. And as we said in our introduction, that's a real termination of our vibration!

So, what do we do? We love ourselves and we love them. However, we might not live with them or regularly associate with them. Everyone deserves to be honored, respected and loved - your family members and yourself. They have their paths and their lessons to learn, just like we do. If a relationship does not honor us, we need to lessen its power within our lives. We honor their path. We might however, choose to take a different one. This is why people of like minds tend to associate with each other. It is also said that One can be judged by the company One keeps. If a culture or a country does not honor your belief system, you owe it to yourself to move. We are obviously blessed in the United States to have freedom of expression. However, the same principle applies to business. How many times have we heard, "That company is making him sick!" Change companies; maybe change professions. Remember that company or that culture also deserves to be honored, but it may not represent your path. We each incarnate with certain lessons to learn. The dominant lesson we all need is to love - ourselves and others - without condition or judgement. Kahlil Gibran in his thoughts on

Gary Schineller

marriage wrote: "But let there be spaces in your togetherness."

From the tears of these decisions love will transcend: love of life, love of God, and love of self...And, a very nice day!

There's more good news. You may have heard this in the media. It is now forecast that for those who are currently fifty years of age, average life expectancy is now 120!

Do you remember in the Bible, man used to live for hundreds of years? He did this with his power of manifestation. This is part of what is being returned to us. Medical science refers to it as the power of prayer. Whichever way we choose to look at it, scientifically or spiritually, the evidence speaks for itself.

Have you also noticed more experiences of déjà vu? Many of us have. This is when we go someplace that we've never been, and it seems as though we've been there before. This is also occurring with people. We are meeting people we've never met, yet it seems we've known them before. This is more good news. And, it will be happening more and more.

Here's an experience I enjoyed. I was driving cross

country with two friends. Neither I, nor anyone in the car, had ever been to Albuquerque, New Mexico. As we were pulling into town, a car stopped next to me at a light, and the driver asked if I knew how to get someplace. Automatically, I began to give him directions! Then I said "never mind it's too complicated; follow me." I made half a dozen turns and took him to the front door. Naturally, my friends were amazed. Quite frankly, so was I, but my Albuquerque experience was just beginning.

We were now back on the main road and looking for a cross street. We had an address of one of my friends'-cousins where we were to spend the night. It was beginning to get dark and we had been driving for quite some time. Of course, someone suggested we stop and ask for directions. Of course, I did not.

It was dark and as we approached an intersection, I said "Let's turn here." There were no street signs at or on this intersection. After going one block, yes, we were on the right street. As we proceeded, there was a large dark opening on the left. I said, "There's the old schoolhouse." The next day we found, set 100 yards back, a large old schoolhouse. We continued to drive until I wanted to stop at a tiny old adobe church on the right. When I said to my

Gary Schineller

friends, "This was my old church," they, shall I say, freaked!

They wanted to know if I was aware of what had been going on. I said, yes, and that I felt there was nothing to fear. I thought we should explore my feelings and see where they led. They agreed, as long as I led the way. That was fine with me.

As we stood next to the side of the church, we were looking up at the free form stained glass windows. One of my friends exclaimed, "That's your image in the window!" Now, we know reflections do not beam upward. There was no lower light. Then we looked directly overhead. This was quite surprising. Earlier on our trip we had been backpacking with some other friends on the John Muir Trail in the Mammoth Lakes region of the High Sierra. While there, I had noticed a tiny cluster of stars that had always appeared in the Northwest sky. I didn't know its name then but referred to it as "my" constellation. I used it as my direction finder for night hiking.

Now we were in New Mexico, which is South and East of the High Sierra. "My" constellation was now directly overhead. Does this make sense? It did not by any logic I knew. Coincidentally, I later learned the name of this constellation to be the Pleiades. I know some of you are smiling right now, but let's continue with Albuquerque.

I felt an urge to walk around the corner and cross the street. As my friends followed, I pointed to the ranch style house on the near corner and said, "Here's my old house!" Coincidentally, the letter "S" was on the front door. We all noticed a beacon of light projecting down on the sidewalk at the corner. Two of us had been engineering majors in college. We could not find or determine the source of that light. We checked every possible angle of refraction or reflection. Still, we didn't know where it was coming from.

The question now was obvious. Do I step into the light? What do you think? I know what I would do today, but at that moment I felt "not-ready." As we turned to walk away, I turned once again to look at the light and it was gone!

Yes, this experience is a little more than your average everyday déjà vu. However, the good news remains. We are all experiencing more déjà vu. We are all experiencing more examples of telepathy. And we are all experiencing heightened abilities of manifestation. Yes, we are having a nice day!

Gary Schineller

9.

Patterns Or
A Body in Motion

——

We learned in physics that a body in motion will tend to stay in motion. The same is true of the patterns of our lives. Whether they are desirable or not, they can be logically expected to continue.

Who do we normally hire: someone who has a stellar track record, or someone down on their luck? Who do we choose to have a relationship with: someone who's been divorced seven times, or someone who knows what they want and why?

Patterns are like living beings. And the first order of life is to survive. Therefore, the pattern in place can be expected to continue unless we consciously choose otherwise. When we can look at the patterns of our lives simply and without judgement, then we are in a healthy state of mind to determine our course.

Let's take a look at a few patterns which I have observed. We'll start with a pleasant or "nice" one. Having grown up in a country environment where everyone knew each other it was normal for me to wave or say hello to just about everyone I passed. Then in college, we created a "nice-gun." It wasn't really a gun, but a walking cane. While stopped at a traffic signal in downtown Buffalo, the person riding on the back of the motorcycle would point it at pedestrians. As we would point it, we would squeeze an imaginary trigger, and playfully sing the word "Nice." Everyone would smile.

Years later I wrote a book called "How to: Have a Nice Day," met the founder of Just Be Nice, Inc., and most recently created "Hello, From My Heart Day," which you'll read about shortly.

Gary Schineller

Does that sound like a pattern? What patterns can you observe in your life? If you choose to examine them, and I hope you do, you may wish to write them in a journal. Doing this tends to remove some of what might be perceived as the "noisy confusion" from our lives. There really are no coincidences, or "coincidinks" as I like to call them. As we begin to acknowledge that, a sense of peace, purpose and meaning begins to unfold.

Here's a short one. Although I grew up in the country, I was born and lived my first five years in New York City. The first meditation class I attended, after living in five different cities, was five blocks from my first home. In a sense, it was like going home again, or as others might say, the birth of a new chapter in my life.

Finding a pattern in one's life can also be very healing. Here's one about Mike, someone I've gotten to know very well. Perhaps there are similarities with someone you know. Mike's story has to do with his parents and the imprints he received from them.

Before I tell this story, it's very important that I reiterate my belief that all events happen *for* us, and not *to* us. Those that accept or acknowledge reincarnation also believe that we choose our parents for the lessons and opportunities they will give us. If you've ever tried to understand why our loving God allows children to be born with illness or affliction, this can give you peace. In this belief system, we - that is our eternal souls - choose what we need to experience. Within or from this point of view we (our souls) seek all experiences leading back to an understanding of our Oneness with God. Personally, I find this to be a fascinating point of view.

Now, back to Mike and the imprints he received. From what I heard, it appeared he had destroyed every significant relationship he'd had with women. Only he didn't really know that, which means he certainly did not know why. However, there was a pattern. He had only been married once, but he had lived with five other women since his divorce. He had two daughters and deeply missed not having a relationship with them. Mike is also what I would describe as a bon vivant.

By the way, his Mom and Dad had been married for 50+ years and he was the first person in his family to get divorced. So, there were no clues there.

After his father crossed over, his brother became the

Gary Schineller

primary source of social interaction for his Mother. After several years his brother asked him to relocate to Florida and help with his Mother. This is where I began to get to know Mike.

For two and a half years Mike chauffeured his mother everywhere. He also built a life for himself. He became an ordained minister and he also appeared on television.

Here's where Mike began to notice a pattern. His mother refused to attend any of his services and was not interested in watching his television show. He also noticed how many of his mother's sentences began with the words, "I don't want you...(to do this or that)." He told me that whenever he would hear that, it began to have the same effect as fingernails on a chalk board. I suggested that we explore why he felt this.

A conversation with his mother proved fruitless and Mike was left with a feeling that in his mother's eyes he did not count for anything. She also began to employ guilt with statements like "you'll be sorry when I'm gone." This is very common and I know most of us have experienced it. Do I hear an, "oh yeah"?

I'll digress for just a moment. When someone feels

threatened by the expectation that they may have done something wrong, what do they do? In the "old school" they attack. They feel that's necessary for self-preservation. Remember, I said patterns have a life. They, too, want to survive. Guilt is a common device used to keep things as they are.

So what do we do? Make sure the person does not feel threatened. Make sure they know you love them without condition or judgement. After all, this is about you, not them. This is much easier said than done. If this person will not accept or honor you, we must recognize that it is their path. We simply do not choose to walk that path any longer. What someone, anyone else thinks of us should have nothing to do with what we think of ourselves. This is part of loving ourselves without judgment.

Now, let's get back to Mike, as he was about to have a revelation. He suddenly recalled how throughout his childhood he was told what his name would have been if he had been born a girl. He also recalled a memory from the age of five or six when his mother had put her bathing cap on him, lipstick on his lips, and her sunglasses. She then paraded him to her sister and her friends. When his dad saw this, he put an immediate stop to it.

Gary Schineller

Mike had not thought about this for many, many years. You might say it was repressed. But now it was all starting to make perfect sense. He was not wanted. Every child wants to be wanted by its parents, but his mother wanted a girl. Obviously, there was nothing he could or would do about that. He, the person he was, could never be what his mother wanted; not then and not now! But, he knew his mother still loved him.

However, Mike is committed to loving without condition or judgement. He also knew he was experiencing this for a reason. That's right. He knew this was happening for him, not to him! Even this. This was an opportunity, not a problem.

For some reason Mike needed to experience not being wanted.

How could he respond to this with love? First love for himself, then love for others. I decided we should explore what his relationships had in common.

In a sudden realization, he knew that in every relationship he had sought beautiful women who were needy. His wife, when he met her, had been told by her doctor that she had two years to live. Twelve years after their marriage

Mike remembers his father asking him if he "counted for anything more than paying the bills" in his family. Is the pattern clear now? It seems he didn't feel worthy of love unless he was needed.

When Mike now looks at his other past partners, he sees they were all needy at the time. They had just been divorced, were going through a divorce, or a parent or loved one had just died. They were all needy. He would be with them until they were well. After they were well, why should they love him? That was the drama he lived. This bright, successful, loving, and happy man actually felt very deep down inside that there was no other reason for someone to love him.

Suddenly, Mike had an explanation for the affairs he had, the drug and alcohol abuse, and the failed relationships. He also knew that this happened for him, not to him. His mother would never knowingly hurt him. This was part of the Divine Plan that he, his mother and his relationships needed to experience. Because of this, there was nothing that needed forgiveness.

Mike now knows, like all of us deserve to, that we are all perfect. He loves himself, his mother and his ex-wife.

Gary Schineller

He is grateful for every person in his life. When his mother chooses to love him for who he is, he is ready. He is a "child of the universe," and "has a right to be here." Mike has released the pattern.

Remember when I said the *Desiderata* fit every life circumstance? Are you a child of the universe? Would you like to see the beautiful intricacy of how patterns can be intertwined. Let's take a look at Marie. I am told every significant male in her life has died prematurely, either literally or figuratively. Her brother committed suicide in his twenties. Her father died at thirty-one. Her uncle was not spoken to for over twenty years. Her first marriage was annulled after two years. Her second marriage ended in divorce after twelve years and she has not spoken to him for over seventeen years. Her quasi-stepfather died at fifty-one. Her grandfather apparently disappeared. Marie is bright, successful, articulate, and from her second marriage, a mother of two. I am told she does not yet recognize this as a pattern. What do you think? By the way, her second husband was Mike!

Patterns do interconnect. She perfectly fit what Mike needed at the time. And Mike, obviously, was perfect for what Marie needed at the time. Will their daughters assume their mother's pattern or choose to create their own? Remember, a body/pattern in motion will tend to stay in motion unless acted upon by an equal or greater force. Our choice can be that force.

By the way, subsequent to Mike completing this work he received a reading from a professional spiritual-intuitive counselor. This was not someone Mike knew or someone who knew him. Shortly into the reading, the counselor said, "Your divorce saved your life!" Events do happen for us!

Imprinting from our parents may also result in affliction or ailment. Here's an example in Allan. Allan is a man of means. He had been extra-ordinarily successful in the corporate world until he suffered vertebrae injury from a whiplash accident. At the time he came to see me he was debilitated by severe migraine headaches.

What's this got to do with parental imprinting? Once again, "events happen for us not to us."

Allan had tried every available means of treatment. Expense was not an issue. Nothing worked. His only relief came from strong drugs that knocked him out. Naturally, his fortune began to disappear and he was not capable

Gary Schineller

of working.

Do you think it was a *coincidink* that we met? The first question I asked was to determine if he really wanted to be well. He certainly did.

To my delight Allan was also a metaphysical student and readily grasped the concept that events happen for us and not to us. It was easy to agree that by finding out why he had experienced this condition he would be well.

First, I measured his chakras. They were all closed, except for his heart.

Allan is centered in love. A week after our first Reiki session, all of his chakras were open except for his sacral or navel chakra. The experiences of pain had lessened significantly.

Now we were getting somewhere. I knew the relief would be temporary until we found the actual cause. Knowing this would probably take a little time, I taught him the ho ho ho, Santa laugh, and asked if he had any orange clothing. Both of these would stimulate his sacral energy. This gave him a tool to deal with any recurring pain.

Next, I asked him if he loved himself. This is a common issue revealed by a closed sacral chakra. I also asked about his relationship with his parents and his wife. Eventually, I discovered that his father had never thought he would amount to anything. His memories of his father were mostly of criticism. Where his father left off, the relationship with his wife continued. She had become exactly like his father.

Do we see a pattern? Just like Mike had experienced the continuation of his mother's role with his wife; Allan had the same chain between his father and his wife. The pain of the migraine headaches could now be seen as happening for Allan not to him. They were the trigger to reveal the much deeper need for healing.

Once we restored the natural energy flow, we could now achieve the healing. First we must all know that we are perfect. As we learned in Chapter One, this is what is meant by "in the image and likeness of God." Second, we must know that everyone else is also! First, we love ourselves. Then, we are capable of truly loving others. If you feel that I am suggesting a path of acceptance, you are only part right. We are going to a place of equality. Acceptance still has elements of judgement. Judgement does not allow

Gary Schineller

the highest energies of love. Whereas a belief in equality, recognizes the perfection in all.

Okay, sounds great. How do we do it? In Allan's case I taught him a meditation in which he viewed scenes from his past with his father and with his wife. Then, once he was visualizing each scene, I asked him to focus or send the energy of love to every person in that scene. Some people do this naturally with their eyes. Others surround the individuals with pink or green light. Still others may choose golden light. Whatever you feel comfortable with is perfect. I also suggested he find an appropriate "pet-name" to call his wife. The power of this technique will be revealed in wonderful depth in the next chapter.

Allan only needed five sessions. He is now reporting that his business has never been better and he's almost completely pain free. He's even getting along better with his wife. Allan was born to win. We are all born to win.

So look for the patterns in your life. Are they in control or are you? In business we use this phrase: "Initiate and Respond." What works in business also works in our personal lives. Conversely, when we are successful in our personal lives, our business always seems to thrive. Once again, there are no coincidences on the way to having a nice day.

Gary Schineller

10.

Part of a Miracle In which Everyone can Participate

—◆～◆—

$\mathcal{T}$he following is a research study taught in Social Psychology. Its value can be seen in personal, spiritual, and global dimensions.

A husband and wife team were researching dynamics of small group behavior. They had two children: a son age thirteen and a daughter age eleven. Both were very popular, had good grades, and excelled in extra curricular activities.

Neither had any nicknames, until they began this study. For a period of thirty days they elected to call their son "Stinky." There was no explanation. Every greeting and every conversation began or ended something like this: "Good Morning, Stinky; or, Did you do your homework, Stinky; or Stinky, how was your day today?" etc.

Within only three weeks their son developed a distinct body odor! This continued and intensified for the remainder of the thirty days. Then they reverted to calling him by his given name. Within seven days the odor disappeared.

The conclusions are both simple and dramatic. We have the tendency to take on or display the characteristics with which we are labeled. Now, let's take another look at our personal relationships. Is there any name-calling or labeling? Are we getting what we're asking for? Should we be surprised when we call somebody something and they behave exactly that way? What would happen if we only described others in glowing and positive terms? Think about the power this principle can have in all aspects of our business and personal lives! Are we having a nice day yet? Maybe it's only three weeks away.

Gary Schineller

I suggested there were global implications to this. Yes, there are. Consider that we all belong to groups. In most cases those groups have names. Let's pick the Taliban for example. If we call the Taliban terrorists, should we expect them to act in any other way? Their name is Taliban. Those that are guilty of crimes should be punished in accordance with the laws of society.

We have learned that our thoughts and words are very, very powerful. And we have learned that they are getting more powerful. Science is reinforcing spirituality and spirituality is reinforcing science. The decision to have a nice day is a decision, and it is ours.

There's a story about God viewing what is happening on Earth. He decides to send a female angel to gather a report. She returns after several days and says to God that 95% of mankind is behaving badly, while only 5% is doing good work. After this, God thinks perhaps He should have a second opinion. He decides to send a male angel to Earth with the same mission. After several days the male angel returns and reports exactly the same information as the female angel: 95% were behaving badly and only 5% were doing good. So God decides to send an email to the 5% that were doing good, so that they might feel rewarded. Do you know what the email said? Seriously, do you know?

Oh, you didn't get the email either?

While none of us that I know have received an email from God, in a way perhaps we just did, because if you're reading this book, you're interested in living in a happier, healthier, more peaceful community. It's a wonderful way for all of us to have a nice day.

11.

Am I on The Right Path

— ❦ —

$\mathcal{F}$or many years during meditation I would ask the question; "Am I on the right path?" Of course the answer would always be yes. And, I promise, whenever any of us asks the same question, the answer will be yes! Makes sense, doesn't it? If we are all perfect and the universe is without judgement we are always on the right path. From a linear point of view the only element for our consideration is how far along that path we presently are.

Two years ago a childhood memory returned to me with all the vividness of yesterday. However, it was not yesterday, it was a memory from when I was age nine. Perhaps you've experienced the same thing.

I grew up in a small country town, perhaps best typified by the two room school house I attended for eight years. When I was nine I put together an association of kids my age from the three surrounding towns. We would meet once a week in a church. We learned about the differences of our various churches. We did some community projects and we had some fun.

I had not thought about it for many years. Yet, suddenly it was returning to my mind over and over again. I could see the faces of the children like it was yesterday. So, while in meditation I asked why it was being shown to me. The answer came in a dream: "Because that's what you're supposed to do now!"

I believe these types of messages happen for all of us. Sometimes we listen. Sometimes we don't. This time I decided to do what I was told, and I started to speak with some friends and pastors. Yes, there was interest in forming an association for all the New Age Churches. New Age Churches, for those who have not attended one, might collectively be known as a place for "truth seekers." People come from every faith and every walk of life. Many also still attend the house of worship of their youth.

However, what I thought was going to happen did not. I thought very simply that many of these churches participated in miracles, and that by associating we would share them and form a library of press releases. This would dispel the mystery of what goes on in a New Age Church. This was the same formula I had used when I was the Chairman of Fund Raising for the Western New York Heart Association. It had resulted then in record contributions and my being named the New York State Volunteer of the Year.

I was wrong. Very few churches participated. However, one of the members, Archbishop Roberto Tocca of the Catholic Church of the Antiochan Rite, encouraged me to stay with it. He had experienced a vision that my work through this association would have national and international impact.

Sometimes we are directed on a particular path. Sometimes we go kicking and screaming. Over the next eighteen months, almost nothing that I engaged in to earn money was fruitful. I was not used to this. I used all my savings and trusted that there was a reason. My needs have always been met In the final analysis I see that if my pattern of corporate success had continued, I would probably have not written this book. And, I certainly would not have had the time to create and run a day that changed the World. Thursday, August 1, 2002, was the first "Hello, From My Heart" Day. We had a wonderful day. We will have many more!

When we experience what some might call failure, we must know and trust that events are happening for us, not to us. Just as I was being guided, we all receive guidance. Sometimes we listen. Sometimes we do what we're told. Do you remember how to make God laugh? The answer is: "Tell him your plans!" I'm here to tell you: when we listen and pay attention, we always have a nice day.

Gary Schineller

12.

Hello From My Heart

On Thursday, August 1, 2002, the people of Tampa Bay, Fl. changed the world. Many of the concepts we have been talking about were proven. Over 750,000 people greeted or were greeted with a smile and the words "Hello, From My Heart." Businesses answered their phones, addressed their emails, and greeted their customers with "Hello, From My Heart." People on the street did the same thing. Several church congregations also participated.

Crime was measured for the eight counties of

Tampa Bay. August 1, 2001 was compared to August 1, 2002. Figures were provided by the respective Sheriff's Departments and a decline of 22% was reported. To insure the statistical reliability, July 31, 2001 was also compared to July 31, 2002. For this day, less than a 1% decline was reported.

Promotion was achieved mostly by an extensive email, telephone and personal appearance campaign. One participant provided a 1.5 million piece email campaign. Each recipient was asked to forward it twenty times. A sample is attached. Maybe you'll recognize it! Response has been received from throughout the United States and almost every continent. There was newspaper coverage the day before. The day of August 1st also featured interviews on several area radio stations as well as TV late news. The NTN network had been announcing it for the thirty days previous. And a major supermarket chain broadcast announcements throughout their stores the entire day.

All of those who participated are genuine heros. Courage was called for, and they delivered. Imagine being the first to say "Hello, From My Heart" to a perfect stranger.

Gary Schineller

Subj: Fwd: "Hello, From My Heart Day" - please forward
Date: 7/30/02 11:57:17 AM Eastern Daylight Time
From:
To:

Gary,

Here's the HTML version of the message that's being mailed today.

Shawn

Forwarded Message:
Subj: "Hello, From My Heart Day" - please forward
Date: 7/30/02 11:55:18 AM Eastern Daylight Time
From:
To:
Sent from the Internet (Details)

Hello, From My Heart Day

HELLO FROM MY HEART

August 1, 2002

Hello, From My Heart Day

Hello, From My Heart,

Can you do something to create Peace? Yes, you can!

On Thursday, August 1st, please greet everyone you meet with a smile and these words: "Hello, From My Heart." Yes, that even includes people you've never met before! Please also answer your telephone with these words: "Hello, From My Heart" followed by your traditional greeting.

Now, please forward this to everyone in your company, your clients, and all your friends. This is being sent to over 1,500,000 people.

Imagine if everyone sends this to just 20 people!

Crime will be measured for August 1st and compared to every other day. We can and we will save lives, reduce violence.

and create a happier more peaceful community. If you want to see the results, you can check our website next week for a full report.

This work is founded in Patriotism, supported by three disciplines of Science, and, of course, motivated by Love.

There is one more thing you can do. Call the Request Line of your favorite radio station and greet the personality with these words: "Hello, From My Heart." Tell them it's "Hello, From My Heart" Day and I wanted to be the first to say "Hello, From My Heart" to you and all your listeners.

That's it. The more people who participate, the greater our results will be...and, it's FREE!

Please remember and be the first on August 1st to say
"Hello, From My Heart"
and the World will thank you.

From my Heart,
Gary Schineller, President
COMMA
www.COMMAUSA.com
1-727-376-0753

P.S. By the way, if you have not tried greeting strangers yet with "Hello, From My Heart," try it! I started when I jog. The response is great!

Throughout the day over 750,000 people were exposed to, or participated in the "Hello, From My Heart" greeting. This means that only 25% of the adults in Tampa Bay gave or received the message. We can also calculate that each of the 25% who heard it, did so an average of 1.3 times during the day.

Never in the history of mankind has such a diversified group achieved such wonderful results. Billions of dollars

Gary Schineller

are spent to lower crime. This did not cost the taxpayers anything. I did not solicit or receive any monies for this work. It required eight months of my time and the courage and commitment of all.

The power of thought, word, and deed were demonstrated! Before "Hello, From My Heart" day, some said that they were already saying "Have a nice day" and other pleasant greetings. And yes, of course, that's wonderful when someone uses those greetings with sincerity. However, most of us remember the first time we heard someone say "Have a nice day." It felt really good then. Why? Because it was powerful. Today, most don't even look us in the eye when they say it. How do we feel today when someone says, "Hi, how are you?" What percentage of those giving or receiving that greeting are really thinking about it? How many times have we said "Good Morning" to someone, only to hear the shortened "morning" in reply? Another not-so-nice example is the "F" word. There was a time when it was powerful. There was a time when using it meant a fight was about to ensue. Today, it's practically part of the vernacular. It has lost its power because those that use it do so, for the most part, without thinking. Now, we have proven the power of our thoughts.

What does "Hello, From My Heart" mean? What does it mean to you? You're right. There are no wrong answers. (The following page will give you an example of what twelve people had to say.)

Here's what some are saying "Hello, From My Heart" means to them.

All answers are perfect!

"I love you." M.S.

"It gives me a reason to smile at someone and give them a compliment." R.N.

"When I say: Hello, from my heart it helps me to look at someone without judgement and with joy." G.S.

"It's an opportunity to go around and spread Love." L.O.

"It means somebody really cares about sharing love." P.E.

"It makes the other person feel obligated to respond nicely." R.B.

"I'm looking forward to answering the telephone with 'Hello, from my heart'; I know it will make everyone feel good." L.C.

"I just did this at a nursing home. Everyone lit up." L.R.

"I'm looking forward to doing this in traffic. I bet we'll have a nicer commute." C.A.

"I've already done this as a jogger. Previously, everyone in my neighborhood ignored each other. Now, everyone smiles." A.H.

"I'm a cashier in a busy store. I hope management let's me do this. It will brighten everyone's day." P.S.

"It means a great big smile and hello." R.S.

What's important is how it makes us feel. And whether you're on the giving or receiving end, you feel good. However we define it, "Hello, From My Heart" is an expression of love. It is also unconditional and without judgement.

What impact does love have on our lives? Yes, it's fun and feels good, but it also reduces stress. Remember, stress is a major contributant to illness. Stress also results in frustration. And frustration, as everyone who has ever taken Psychology 101 remembers, causes aggression. As we all know, frustration is everywhere. Consider the crime rates. Today, we even have Road Rage. These are all born of frustration and expressed with aggression.

I remember one office manager who said she would not say "Hello, From My Heart" because that would be an expression she would reserve for her husband or sweetheart. (I didn't ask if that meant two different peo-ple!) To me it was the perfect answer. When we say "Hello, From My Heart" it is an expression of unconditional love. The key word here is expression. When we express love versus just saying it, we are very powerful.

One very good question I was asked had to do with who got the message. They wondered since crime was reduced, were they actually saying "Hello, From My Heart" to would-be criminals? Not necessarily. While certain individuals' stress or frustration was definitely lowered, an even more important component was at work.

Do you remember the story of the 100th Monkey from Chapter Two? This is why it is so important to have as many people as possible participate. It has to do with energy. You might call it good *vibrations*! Einstein showed with "Energy = Mass x The Speed of Light(squared)" that *everything* in the material world is energy and part of what he called the Universal Energy Field. Courtesy of this discovery, students of Quantum Physics have proven that the properties of subatomic particles respond directly to the thoughts of the observer. This confirms that the mind is part of this energy field and is able to influence it.

Gary Schineller

Our premise was that the use of a powerful phrase - "Hello, From My Heart" by a very large number of people would generate enough energy to lower crime. Based on the individual county reports, it can be concluded that where the greatest number of people participated, the greatest results were achieved.

From my knowledge of mass communications we can expect the maximization of our results to be attained when we achieve a minimum reach of 50% of the population a minimum of three times each. This means that at least half the people will say or hear "Hello, From My Heart" a minimum of three times on the next "Hello, From My Heart" Day..

Here's an example of the power of collective consciousness, which I suspect all of us have seen, but few remember where it started. The date was August 1969, thirty-three years prior to the first "Hello, From My Heart" Day. This number may be significant to you.

This happened at an outdoor concert. It was raining and was forecast to continue. That is until all 500,000 in attendance began chanting the words "no-rain." Also, everyone held up to the heavens a candle, a lighter, or matches.

The rain stopped.

Today, we witness at concerts all over the world audiences holding up to the heavens little flashlights or lighters. As I said, most don't remember, but perhaps you've guessed; the custom was born at Yasgood's farm in Woodstock, N.Y.

Perhaps thirty-three years from today, people the world over will be saying "Hello, From My Heart," and it won't matter if they don't recall it was born August 1, 2002 in Tampa Bay, Fl. We can then live in a happier, healthier, more peaceful World community. And, we'll all be having a really nice day.

"Hello, From My Heart" Day will now be held worldwide on September 11th. What are you going to say on that day? Yes, "Hello, From My Heart." Who are you going to say it to: EVERYONE. And the World will thank you.

Now, that's a really nice day.

Gary Schineller

13.

Go Placidly...

—◆—◆—

The work of "Hello, From My Heart" will continue. It is blessed and so are we. Plans continue to be developed to expand its nationwide and worldwide reach. I hope you will join us.

This does not mean that we will not face many challenges along the path. We will. I am sure you can imagine the number of people who looked at me as though I had a bird on my head when I began this work. Some actually laughed at me. Others told me they would participate, only to do nothing. Still others just didn't return telephone calls.

Yes, there were times I questioned my faith. After all, we are human. However, by practicing what we have been discussing, I was able to stay strong. When we practice these tools, this discipline, we also allow ourselves to feel the rewards of the universe.

As you know, I jog most mornings. It's a marvelous time for me to refresh and recharge. It's actually quite meditative. And, it's a time when I receive Divine messages.

This is a story about two such mornings. I had been experiencing rejection from several sources. The first morning, while I was jogging through a somewhat soggy section of the golf course, I was seeking strength and inspiration by repeating my mantra:

I Am Love

I Love

I Am Loved

I was also asking God if I could please have a sign of his support for my work. The next day as I jogged through the same area, my footprints were in bloom! These grass footprints were brighter, greener, and taller. Now, I am sure

Gary Schineller

there is a botanical reason to explain this. However, I have never, before or after, seen the same effect. I was in awe! Do you think I received inspiration and strength? The same is there for you.

If this work has touched you and you really would like to have a nice day, I suggest you read this book three times within the first month of your first reading. Participate with it. Involve yourself. New insight and applications to your own life will become clear.

Keep a journal of your dreams and revelations.

Then read this book again in one month. Are you practicing the I AM? Are you aware of what you are taking possession of and releasing? Are you loving yourself?

Continue to read this work monthly until you have noticed a sense of peace and joy become part of your every day life. Then you might like to give your book away.

As we do this work, we receive many blessings. "Hello, From My Heart" is about love. It's also about the Golden Rule "Do unto others as you would have them do unto you." There is a version of the Golden Rule within every religion on the planet. God is within every religion on the planet. It's that simple. We are One.

It starts with loving ourselves. If you engage in the "should-ofs," eliminate them. Love yourself.

"You are a child of the universe"

"Do not distress yourself"

"Be gentle with yourself"

"Go placidly amid the noise and haste"

"Whether or not it is clear to you,
no doubt the universe is unfolding as it should"

We are perfect expressions of God. Events do not happen to us, but for us. Enjoy that. Enjoy yourself. "Hello, From My Heart."

Gary Schineller

Power Quiz

— • • —

Scientists tell us we use 10-12% of our brains.

However, everyone's abilities are increasing. Record your answers once again, and see

HOW MUCH OF YOUR POWER YOU ARE USING.

Mark the answer that most clearly represents your belief.
Please remember there are no wrong answers.

1   (a) I always have a good day.
    (b) I always try to make it a good day.
    (c) I have no control over whether or not I have a good day.

2   (a) I hate one person.
    (b) I hate a few people.
    (c) I don't hate anyone.

3 (a) I am a happy person.
   (b) I try to be a happy person.
   (c) I get mad once in a while.

4 (a) I feel worried about the future.
   (b) I live in the moment and am grateful.
   (c) I wish I could turn back the clock.

5 (a) I have the courage to fight for my convictions.
   (b) I like to remain neutral.
   (c) I believe in equality.

6 (a) I get sick once in a while.
   (b) I am always perfect.
   (c) I have a recurring condition.

7 (a) I am always on time.
   (b) I am sorry when I arrive late.
   (c) I don't care if I am late.

8 (a) I sometimes worry about money
   (b) I always have enough money.
   (c) I don't care about money.

9 (a) My life can sometimes be described as "Why does this keep happening to me?"
   (b) I look at all events as happening for me versus to me.
   (c) I desire a healthy relationship.

Gary Schineller

10 (a) What others think of me has nothing to do with what I think of myself.

   (b) I am willing to look at things from other's point of view.

   (c) I feel guilty or ashamed once in a while

To receive a score determining how much of your power you are using, answers to a completed Power Quiz may be sent to Gary at Gary@HelloFromMyHeart.com. Please place the words "FREE POWER QUIZ ANALY-SIS" in the subject. All results are confidential.

www.ingramcontent.com/pod-product-compliance
Lightning Source LLC
Chambersburg PA
CBHW032102080426
42733CB00006B/379